MOUNTAIN STATES
STATES
Foraging

MOUNTAIN STATES
Foraging

115 wild and flavorful edibles
from alpine sorrel to wild hops

BRIANA WILES

TIMBER PRESS
Portland, Oregon

Frontispiece: Wandering off trail my whole life has done me a world of good, especially when it comes to foraged finds.

Published in 2016 by Timber Press, Inc.
Hachette Book Group
1290 Avenue of the Americas
New York, NY 10104

timberpress.com

Timber Press, Inc., is a subsidiary of Workman Publishing Co., Inc., a subsidiary of Hachette Book Group, Inc.

Printed in China on responsibly sourced paper
Fourth printing 2022

Text and cover design by Benjamin Shaykin

Library of Congress Cataloging-in-Publication Data

Names: Wiles, Briana, author.
Title: Mountain states foraging: 115 wild and flavorful edibles from alpine
    sorrel to wild hops / Briana Wiles.
Other titles: 115 wild and flavorful edibles from alpine sorrel to wild hops
Description: Portland, Oregon: Timber Press, 2016. | Includes index.
Identifiers: LCCN 2015045861 | ISBN 9781604696783 (pbk.)
Subjects: LCSH: Wild plants, Edible—West (U.S.) | Wild plants,
    Edible—Alberta. | Wild plants, Edible—Saskatchewan.
Classification: LCC QK98.5.A1 W53 2016 | DDC 581.6/32—dc23
    LC record available at http://lccn.loc.gov/2015045861

A catalog record for this book is also available from the British Library.

*To my husband, Briant, and our son,
Salix—for bringing me forever closer
to the wild treasures in life*

Contents

Preface

How can I forget my Italian grandfather's love for food? He had a garden plot with a variety of grapes, figs, plums, eggplants, tomatoes, and peppers, all staples of his old country. I fondly remember feral pears and apples scattered on Grandpa's dashboard. I can taste Grandma's giardiniera and see the giant jars of pickles from the harvests lined up in the basement. I come from a family who loved to celebrate food, and those roots give me passion for everything I do. Whether it's the garden I plant and feed my family from or the shrubs that I forage, I am connected to my family's traditions wholeheartedly.

Foraging for food has a feast of fans already. A movement is happening to rewild, regain, and revolutionize our tarnished food system. We want to eat local produce and to know where our food comes from. This can mean getting to know local farmers, food producers, and ranchers. We can also empower ourselves by being gatherers and heading into the woods, not just for the free food but also for respite. Foraging is about returning to the land with humbled hands. Let's learn to take the time to sustainably prune the plants of the forest, spread seeds of the fields, and ensure the success of native plants by tending nature's garden.

Spending time in nature, with keen eyes, a slow pace, and a soft impact, is a good thing, but even better is to connect our feet and fingers with the matters of the earth in a way that brings us nutrients. Just a pinch of wild in each dish is a success to celebrate, a way to start incorporating the freedom of foraging.

It is a true blessing to live in a rural town in central Colorado. Here, I am surrounded by different climates within an arm's reach: moist mountains, arid sagebrush, and riparian havens. The sands of Utah and the metropolitan Front Range are only four hours away, providing me with yet another variety of plants not found near my home. I can't help but always be prepared to make a few gathering stops on the way.

I chose the plants for this book based on my personal taste preferences and my experience with each plant as food. My wish is to provide the reader with the skills to seek out and harvest a plant with a sustainable mindset and then to preserve your harvest and prepare these feral foods for feast.

My hope is not that this book will sit on a shelf or table but rather that it will somehow land, open, in the hands of a bored child or an adult waiting anxiously for time to pass. When they leave that spot, I want them to greet the lamb's quarters, dandelions, and salsify with an irresistible urge to pick a leaf and taste it. This is how foraging lures you in, takes hold of your whole being, and welcomes you to the wild side.

Teaching my son, Salix, to forage for wild strawberries before his first birthday. Every child should know the true flavor of strawberries and experience the joy of finding food from the land.

Introduction:
Foraging High and Low

Sit down with this book alongside a weedy sidewalk or a meandering trail among the plants that grow in your habitat. Tickle your palate with wildflowers and colorful fruits that can coexist in the kitchen among your usual dishes. There is something very special about connecting your hands and taste buds to a successfully identified wild edible.

The start of a spring salad is a bowl of violets and bluebells waiting to be washed and trimmed up to use in a spring salad.

Mountain West

The states and provinces of the mountain west—Colorado, Wyoming, Montana, Utah, Nevada, Idaho, the eastern sides of Washington and Oregon, and north into the southernmost parts of Alberta and Saskatchewan—are uniquely their own, with high mountain peaks, broad valleys, high deserts, and lush pockets of forests. Elevation plays a huge role in seasonal changes and precipitation here, with mountains ranging from about 2,000 feet to over 14,000 feet. In these parts, a forager can chase seasons from the low plains all the way to the high country. It can be a bit tricky at times to precisely plan out your harvest because of this. Berry season may be just beginning in the highlands while pickings are already slimming in the low-lying basins.

Within hours of travel by car, the scenery will have changed multiple times, fluctuating between stands of chokecherry, aspen, or scrub oak. Upon gaining elevation, it changes to woodlands, where one might find sweet root, thimbleberry, or cow parsnip. Open meadows may be full of sweet clover, wild chives, and sunflowers, while the desert lowlands provide the wild foodie with Mormon tea, prickly pear, and piñon. The land seems endless here, where the mountains soar and the rivers carve through. Let this book be your friend while you explore nature's regional gift of foods.

How to Let This Book Guide You

Plants are listed alphabetically by the most common name used in the area. Botanical names of plants are shown in italics, distinguishing plants to genus and often to species, as a binomial. These scientific names are used to more precisely identify plants; common names, confusingly, are often used for more than one plant.

Always use more than one reference to identify a plant. Although this book offers photos and clear indicators for recognizing each plant, you will still need a precise key for distinguishing certain species. I provide general guidance for where each plant may be found growing, but again, this can be quite variable throughout our region.

Each entry lists the edible parts of the plant, along with ideas of how to gather and prepare these feral foods for feast. Food preservation of most plants is discussed, for that longer-lasting bounty that will stock your cupboards and freezer.

Plants vary from being common weeds that can be found in gardens, such as purslane, to crabapples, lindens, and other trees that line the streets of most towns. No need to worry if you can't escape to the wilderness; plenty of wild plants are growing right outside your back door.

Plants to avoid

It is always wise to learn your poisons first before you begin consuming wild foods. These plants are commonly found throughout the states and provinces of the mountain west.

Take a good look at the shape of water hemlock (*Cicuta* species) leaves; they are the first thing you want to be able to recognize on these toxic plants. Also, become familiar with identifying their ribbed and plumply crescent-shaped seeds.

Meadow death camas (*Toxicoscordion venenosum*), pictured, and mountain death camas (*Anticlea elegans*) should never be consumed.

Poison hemlock (*Conium maculatum*) can grow very tall, taking over entire fields. Learn to identify it, and never eat any part of this plant.

Larkspurs (*Delphinium* species) are beautiful but not edible.

All parts of monkshood (*Aconitum columbianum*) are poisonous and should not be consumed in any quantity.

Baneberries (*Actaea* species) can be red or white. Either way, avoid them.

Young leaves of golden banner (*Thermopsis* species) can resemble alfalfa, sweet clover, and other clovers.

See those "leaves of three"? Poison ivy (*Toxicodendron* species) is a plant you do not want to grab hold of.

The light green shoots of false hellebore (*Veratrum* species) should not be confused with twisted stalk.

Forage safely

Before considering any plant for consumption, be aware of possible cautions, contraindications to medicines, and poisonous look-alikes of that plant. Again, use multiple guidebooks or plant keys to identify plants with certainty. Be sure to check if a plant's entry has a cautionary warning before consuming any plant you read about in this book. Never touch or taste any part of a plant you are uncertain about; even a few seeds of poison hemlock or water hemlock can be fatal. Some people have an allergic reaction to sesquiterpenoid compounds, which are present in varying amounts in most plants in the daisy or sunflower family (Asteraceae)— small bites until you know for certain you are not one of them! It is always best to sample a small amount of any wild food you have not eaten before. And be aware of the plants that surround you. Some plants can be very irritating to the skin; poison ivy, for example, is one you definitely do not want to grab hold of. With other, even edible plants, like cow parsnip, you run a small risk of dermatitis. If your skin gets sap on it, a burn can occur; again, always read the cautions.

A word about contaminants

We are very privileged to have made our home in the mountain west, where the land is wide open and free from crowds; however, we still need to pay attention to where we choose to gather. The soil in populated cities and even rural communities can harbor chemicals from herbicides and pesticides and heavy metals from mining and factories, along with other contaminants. Many weedy edibles such as ox-eye daisies or burdock can be the target of eradication. If a plant looks deformed or yellowed and brown when it should be green, it has probably been sprayed with an herbicide; don't collect near there. Stay far from roads, railways, municipal facilities, golf courses, and landscaped buildings, as these are generally highly sprayed areas.

Be leery of gathering near cattle ranches or farms. The waters that flow through them can carry fertilizers, manure, and many other contaminants that then leach into waterways downstream. Poor land use practices have meant the erosion of many of these riparian areas, which in turn causes shallow, slow-moving, warm waters. Such environments mean the water has a greater potential to host E. coli, salmonella, liver flukes, and other contaminants. Don't harvest water-loving plants from the shores of rivers or reservoirs that are contaminated or polluted by mining, factories, or agriculture.

The Sustainable Harvest: Foraging Ethics

The golden rule of foraging wild plants is to be more than certain of the plant you wish to consume. Learn to identify the plant before you even touch it, much less start harvesting from it. Learn to gain trust between yourself and Mother Nature, but always lean toward caution with anything new.

Be a steward of the land

The secret to successful, ethical foraging isn't how much you bring home: it's conducting yourself in such a way that no one would ever know you had passed through. Harvest only what is needed for a meal (and perhaps a bit for the pantry), in a way that tends the earth. If you are digging up roots, understand this means that spring beauties and many other tuberous plants will not regenerate, while dandelions will grow again if a small piece of root is left in the ground. Harvest roots and tubers only from areas that are abundant in growth; small patches should never be touched. Find seeds of the same plant and place them in the hole before covering, in hopes it will grow a plant ten times greater than the one you harvested with love and care. Fill the empty space where life once grew with the dirt you removed, and some leaves for composting, leaving the land, to all appearances, untouched. All these are respectful gestures to the plant.

I always look for fallen branches instead of ever taking one away from a tree; small trimmings are okay if you spread that harvest out through many trees. Look for places where people have removed a tree or are doing trail maintenance; great timing can get you a bounty of conifer boughs. If picking tree buds or tips, move through many trees; do not harvest from only one.

Never pick all the leaves from a single plant; take under a third of what the plant has to offer. Removing more will weaken the plant and not allow it to have a successful life cycle. Flowers too should be picked with care, as they are the source of reproduction; always leave plenty behind, and allow many plants to remain fully intact.

Keep it legal

Public lands dominate much of the rural west, which is great for the forager, but be aware: restrictions often apply. Each public land agency, such as Bureau of Land Management (BLM), United States Fish and Wildlife Services, and national and provincial park services, has different rules and regulations about harvesting on their lands. In addition to federal or Crown lands, states and provinces also manage open spaces and have their own set of rules. Check in with your local office to learn what the regulations are.

Be aware of private properties, such as ranches and mining claims. It is your duty to know if you are trespassing. Even within neighborhoods or down alleyways, always ask permission to harvest from someone else's property.

Eat the invaders

Many of the common weeds mentioned in this book are introduced species that are not considered invasive. These plants can usually be harvested more freely without worry of taking too much, as they grow pretty abundantly. Check your state or provincial noxious weed list (easily found online) and know the invasive plants. It is worth knowing which plants are sprayed in your area. A simple call to the forest service or your local department or ministry of transportation can be a good place to start when trying to find this information.

Gearing Up: Handy Tools and Foraging Garb

When heading out for a harvest day, one should always be layered and prepared for a change in weather. It can even be wise to have a change of clothes in the car, but maybe it's just me who wades rivers fully clothed.

Seasons are constantly shifting, especially if you plan on gaining elevation to forage.

A hefty basket of stinging nettles, carefully harvested with gloves and pruners.

Garbling plants

To garble a plant is to pick it apart for the parts that are useful. For example, garbling elderflowers or -berries would mean that you pick off only the flowers or fruit, keeping all the stems out of your harvest pile (the fresh stems of elderberry are toxic).

It also means going through your harvest basket and making sure that you gathered only the plants you meant to harvest, removing any plants that are not identified or debris that is undesirable to eat.

Garbling the round silicles of clasping pepperweed off the stalks and into a bowl.

The temperature will always be slightly cooler and possibly breezier the higher you go. The exact opposite is usually the case if you are heading lower; in that case, expect it to be much hotter and more arid.

Wear shoes that allow you to walk up a scree field or through a rocky river. An all-terrain shoe will do, or perhaps a minimalist barefoot shoe is more appealing. Some people really like to feel the land, while others prefer protection; choose what suits you. Rubber or suede boots can be a nice way to tromp around rivers and wetlands, while bare feet or sandals could be totally appropriate for grassy or sandy knolls. Always have a raincoat and sunglasses, two essentials in the mountain west, where if it's not intensely sunny, then it is probably raining or snowing. The harsh climate of the summer is the perfect reminder to cover up from the sun. Wear a hat and light long layers, and use a sunblock on exposed skin. Altitude makes the sun fiercer, and our bodies work harder, so always have enough water for drinking. Hydration makes a happy harvester.

Baskets, pruners, belts, and satchels are among a forager's favorite things. It is nice to have the essential utensils within arm's reach, which means a belt or satchel are handy for carrying pruners, knives, and digging tools. Paper bags, pillow cases, baskets, or muslin bags are great for gathering fresh plant matter; it lets them air out while you continue to harvest and garble. Using plastic bags or containers traps in moisture and can make your harvest go bad quickly from mold and rot. Glass jars or plastic containers are needed when collecting berries, so your harvest does not go mushy.

Processing Plant Matter

Now that you have found your wild edibles, you need to prep them for cooking, eating, or storing for later use.

Winnowing

Winnowing is the process of removing seeds from the bracts or casings that enclose them. Try this with small seeds like alfalfa, amaranth, western blue flax, and lamb's quarters. To begin winnowing, get outside with your dried seedheads and, standing over a bucket, take a scoop of them in one hand. Then take both hands and rub them together slowly; this lets the desired seeds fall into the bucket, a foot or two below, while simultaneously allowing the chaff and other plant debris to blow away in the wind.

Dehydrating and drying

The process of drying or dehydrating plants is a great way to store food for later ventures in your wild edible culinary experience. Don't worry if you are not equipped with a fancy dehydrator. Your kitchen table, oven, shed, or broken-down car will work just fine.

If you have a dehydrator, use your lowest settings for leaves and flowers. Roots, berries, and sliced fruits may be able to withstand a warmer temperature. Always use the lowest temperature setting if using an oven, which is generally around 170 degrees Fahrenheit.

My favorite way to dry plant matter is to spread it all out on mesh screens or stretched-out linen sheets; the herb can then be jostled every so often to keep the drying evenly distributed. Laying your garbled plants flat on parchment paper that is spread over a table will also work; just remember to rotate the sides of your plant matter so that they dry evenly. Try to find a place outside that is in the shade, so the plants do not scorch in the sun. Doing the drying inside is fine but can sometimes result in a home bug infestation.

Settling on terms

Plants have characteristics all their own, and learning some easy terminology will help you to identify which to gather. Because plants bear leaves most of the harvesting season, even without flowers or fruits, leaves are key to identifying and distinguishing plants. Take a look at the shape of the leaves, and the pattern in which the leaves are arranged. For a better botanical understanding, here are some examples of common leaf arrangements, shapes, and margins.

OPPOSITE Mint leaves grow in pairs, joining at the same node on the stem.

WHORLED Cleavers has three or more leaves arranged around one node on a stem.

ALTERNATE The leaves of twisted stalk grow along the stem, one at each node.

ROSETTE Tumble mustard leaves are arranged around the base of the plant, forming a dense mat of leaves on the ground.

COMPOUND Red clover leaves are separated into three leaflets.

OBLONG Showy milkweed leaves are longer than they are wide.

PINNATE Wild licorice has a compound leaf with opposite leaflets along the axis.

LANCEOLATE Stinging nettle leaves are longer than they are wide, with a speared tip.

ENTIRE Lilac leaves are smooth around the margin.

OVATE Plantain has oval or egg-shaped leaves.

SERRATED The margins of Oregon grape leaves are jagged or toothed.

PALMATE Cow parsnip veins radiate from a central point into lobes.

LOBED Scrub oak leaves have deep rounded margins.

Timing Your Forage:
A Guide to Seasonal Harvests

Figuring out your jive with nature and a habitual routine for gathering wild plants for food and preservation will pay off in the years to come. Start small and don't overwhelm yourself with trying to find every edible plant in the forest. Meet and greet a few plants each season and visit them throughout the harvesting year to memorize when they first sprout, flower, or fruit. Eventually, you will have dried berries, herbs, or other preserved wild foods from the previous years' harvests to go along with the flowers and fresh greens of a new spring forage.

It is good practice to have your own journal of foraging locations, keeping notes of plants by name and date, and taking pictures of their stages of growth. This will help with future harvest planning, knowing the seasons by what you experience, not by what a book tells you. Due to the extreme elevation variability of the mountain west, seasons "happen" at equally variable times; plants know only what the weather is telling them. Spring may start in March in some places, while it will not truly arrive until late May in others. Continue to visit the same locations over and over again throughout the year, a few times each season. This is how you learn the plants and their life cycle.

Make a plan on a winter's day, plotting out the plants you already know and welcoming a few new ones to find come spring. Learn to recognize where the plants grow, and when they put forth shoots, leaves, and flower buds. Stalk the wooded hills with wide eyes and a slow pace.

Early Spring

Early spring in the Rockies can be a toss-up—full of snowstorms or unbelievably warm days. Luckily, collecting from trees can be done in any kind of weather. Spring catkins, twigs, and barks are at the perfect stage for harvesting. The spring sap is running through the trunk and limbs, getting ready to turn buds into leaves and flowers.

The lowlands and deserts of the mountain west provide young yucca stalks that look like giant asparagus. Young rosettes of mustard leaves and tasty roots like salsify are best while the plant's energy is localized close to the earth. Flowers are beginning to blossom a few thousand feet lower than where the snow is still lingering in high mountains. Forests and open meadows harbor more tubers, budding flowers, and unfurling young leaves prime for harvesting.

It may look sparse, but spring in the mountain meadows eventually brings young leaves of glacier lilies, stinging nettles, violets, mountain candytuft, and spring beauties.

Where to Find Early Spring Plants

Open Meadows, Disturbed Soils, or Forest Edges

blue mustard: leaves, stalks, flowers

Brandegee's onion: leaves, flowers, bulbs

burdock: shoots, leaves, stalks, roots

chicory: leaves, roots

dandelion: leaves, flower buds, flowers, roots

filaree: leaves, roots

glacier lily: leaves, bulbs

lamb's quarters: leaves

mallow: leaves, stems, roots

mountain candytuft: leaves, stalks, flowers

mountain parsley: leaves, roots

nodding onion: leaves, stalks, bulbs

orache: leaves

ox-eye daisy: leaves

pennycress: leaves, flowers

pepperweed: leaves

plantain: leaves

salsify: shoots, leaves, roots

shepherd's purse: leaves, flowers, seedpods

tansy mustard: leaves, flower buds, seedpods

tumble mustard: leaves, flower buds

white clover: leaves

whitetop: leaves

wild hops: shoots

wild lettuce: leaves

wild licorice: shoots, roots

wild strawberry: leaves, flowers

yarrow: leaves

Desert, Among Sagebrush, or Rocky Soil

balsamroot: leaves, stems, roots

juniper: leaves, fruit

Mormon tea: stems

piñon: needles, resin

prickly pear: pads, flower buds, flowers

yucca: stalks

Near Wetlands, Riverbanks, Lakesides, or Bogs

asparagus: shoots

cattail: shoots, roots

cottonwood: buds, bark, twigs

stinging nettle: shoots, leaves

veronica: leaves

watercress: leaves

wild mint: leaves

wintercress: leaves

Woodlands or Partially Shaded Places

aspen: buds, bark, twigs

chickweed: leaves, stems, flowers

Douglas fir: needles, resin

fir: needles, resin

fireweed: shoots

pine: needles, resin

spring beauty: leaves, roots

spruce: needles, resin

sweet root: roots, leaves

thimbleberry: shoots, leaves

violet: leaves

wood sorrel: leaves

Mid- to Late Spring

The rivers are raging at this time of year. Mid- to late spring is when peak runoff flows from the winter's melting snow. Riparian areas swell with the flood of water, and the leaves of young plants are crisp for harvesting. Many of theses plants tend to get bitter and tough or dry up during the summer months, an example being dock. Many flowers—dwarf bluebells, mountain parsley, prickly pear, and others—have blossomed.

Asparagus spears may be growing past their prime, while thimbleberry shoots can still be sought in the wooded mountains. Find tasty Brandegee's onion bulbs and gather spruce tips while the weather is still cool at night but warming more and more each day.

Where to Find Mid- to Late Spring Plants

Open Meadows, Disturbed Soils, or Forest Edges

alfalfa: leaves

amaranth: leaves

beebalm: leaves

bistort: leaves, roots

bluebells: leaves, flowers

blue mustard: leaves, stalks, flowers, seedpods

Brandegee's onion: leaves, flowers, bulbs

burdock: leaves, roots

chicory: leaves, roots

crabapple: flowers

dandelion: leaves, flowers, roots

dock: leaves, roots

filaree: leaves, roots

glacier lily: leaves, flowers, bulbs

lamb's quarters: leaves, stems

lilac: flowers

linden: leaves

mallow: leaves, flowers, roots

mariposa lily: flowers, bulbs

mountain candytuft: leaves, stalks, flowers, seedpods

mountain parsley: leaves, roots

mulberry: leaves

nodding onion: leaves, stalks, bulbs

orache: leaves

ox-eye daisy: leaves

pennycress: leaves, flowers

pepperweed: leaves, seedpods

plantain: leaves

raspberry: leaves

red clover: leaves, flowers

salsify: shoots, leaves, roots

sheep sorrel: leaves

shepherd's purse: leaves, flowers, seedpods

showy milkweed: shoots

stonecrop: leaves, stems

strawberry blite: leaves

sweet clover: shoots, leaves

tansy mustard: leaves, flower buds, seedpods

thistle: stalks

tumble mustard: leaves, flower buds

white clover: leaves

whitetop: leaves, stalks, flower buds

A basket of Douglas fir tips gathered in late spring, while they are soft, sweetly citrus flavored, and a shade of neon green.

wild caraway: leaves, roots
wild chives: leaves, flower
   buds

wild hops: leaves
wild lettuce: leaves
wild licorice: shoots, roots

wild strawberry: leaves
yarrow: leaves

Desert, Among Sagebrush, or Rocky Soil

alpine sorrel: leaves
balsamroot: leaves, stems,
   roots
juniper: leaves

king's crown: shoots
Mormon tea: stems
piñon: needles, resin

prickly pear: pads, flower
   buds, flowers
yucca: stalks

Near Wetlands, Riverbanks, Lakesides, or Bogs

angelica: roots
cattail: shoots, flower spikes
cottonwood: bark, twigs,
   catkins, cambium

stinging nettle: shoots, leaves
twisted stalk: shoots
veronica: leaves, stems,
   flowers

watercress: leaves, flowers
wild mint: leaves, stems
wintercress: leaves

Woodlands or Partially Shaded Places

aspen: bark, twigs
chickweed: leaves, stems,
   flowers
chokecherry: flowers
cleavers: leaves, stems
cow parsnip: leaves
Douglas fir: young tips,
   needles, resin
elderberry: flowers
fir: young tips, needles, resin

fireweed: shoots, leaves
northern bedstraw: leaves,
   stalks
pine: needles, resin, pollen
spring beauty: leaves, stems,
   flowers, roots
spruce: young tips, needles,
   resin
sweet root: leaves, flowers,
   roots

thimbleberry: shoots, leaves
violet: leaves, flowers
wild grape: leaves, tendrils
wild rose: flower buds
wood sorrel: leaves, flowers

Summer

The heat of summer is welcome in the high Rockies, where the growing season is a mere three months. At lower elevations, the arid heat of the summer months provides a longer growing season for wild plums, feral apples, and other fruit trees.

Monsoon season sweeps in; daily rains occur in the high country during July, giving the plants the boost they need for fruiting berries. It is best to wake up with the sun and gather while it is dry in the morning, as it can become a muddy mess by mid-afternoon. Be careful of lightning storms while hiking high in the mountains and flash floods while in canyon lands. In certain places it is not uncommon to see a snow shower on the mountain peaks in early July.

Summertime in the mountains provides a bounty of wild edibles and the most picturesque views.

Wildflowers are breathtaking, making it more than enjoyable to hike through meadows in search of wild strawberries and nodding onion. Aromatics of plants like beebalm, pineapple weed, and hyssop are superior during the height of summer.

Where to Find Summer Plants

Open Meadows, Disturbed Soils, or Forest Edges

alfalfa: leaves, flowers, seeds

amaranth: leaves, seeds

beebalm: leaves, flower buds, flowers

bistort: leaves, flowers, roots

black walnut: green hulls

bluebells: leaves, flowers

blue mustard: seedpods

Brandegee's onion: leaves, flowers, bulbs

burdock: stalks

chicory: flowers

dandelion: flowers

goldenrod: leaves, flower buds, flowers

ground cherry: fruit

lamb's quarters: leaves

linden: flowers, nuts

mallow: leaves, flowers, seedpods

mariposa lily: flowers, bulbs

mountain parsley: leaves

mulberry: fruit

nodding onion: leaves, stalks, flowers, bulbs

orache: leaves, seeds

ox-eye daisy: leaves, flower buds, flowers

pennycress: seedpods

pepperweed: seedpods, roots

pineapple weed: leaves, flowers

plantain: leaves, seeds

purslane: leaves, stems, flowers, seeds

raspberry: leaves, flowers, fruit

red clover: leaves, flowers

salsify: shoots, leaves, flower buds

serviceberry: fruit

sheep sorrel: leaves

showy milkweed: flower buds, flowers, seedpods

smooth sumac: fruit

sow thistle: shoots, flower buds, leaves

stonecrop: leaves, stems, flowers

strawberry blite: leaves, flowers

sunflower: flower buds

sweet clover: leaves, flowers, seeds

thistle: stalks

tumble mustard: seedpods

western blue flax: seeds

white clover: leaves, flowers

whitetop: flowers, seedpods

wild caraway: leaves, flowers, seeds, roots

wild chives: leaves, flowers

wild hops: leaves, strobiles

wild lettuce: stalks, flower buds

wild strawberry: fruit

yarrow: leaves, stalks, flowers

Desert, Among Sagebrush, or Rocky Soil

alpine sorrel: leaves

balsamroot: seeds

cota: leaves, stems, flowers

juniper: leaves

king's crown: leaves, flowers

Mormon tea: stems

Oregon grape: fruit

prickly pear: pads, fruit

piñon: needles

skunkbush: fruit

yucca: flower buds, flowers, seedpods

Near Wetlands, Riverbanks, Lakesides, or Bogs

angelica: stalks, seeds

cattail: shoots, flower spikes, pollen

stinging nettle: leaves, seeds

veronica: leaves, stems, flowers

watercress: leaves, seedpods

wild mint: leaves, flowers

Woodlands or Partially Shaded Places

blueberry: fruit

chickweed: leaves, stems, flowers

chokecherry: bark, twigs, fruit, nuts

cleavers: leaves, stems, seeds

cow parsnip: stalks, flower buds, seeds

Douglas fir: needles

elderberry: flowers, fruit

fir: needles

fireweed: stalks, flower buds, flowers

golden currant: fruit

gooseberry: fruit

hawthorn: fruit

hyssop: leaves, flowers

miner's lettuce: leaves, stems, flowers

mountain gooseberry: fruit

New Mexico locust: flowers

northern bedstraw: leaves, flowers

pine: needles

spruce: needles

sweet root: leaves, seeds

thimbleberry: fruit

violet: leaves

wax currant: fruit

wild grape: fruit

wild plum: fruit

wild rose: flower buds, flowers

Wolf's currant: fruit

wood sorrel: leaves, flowers, seedpods

Fall

Fall either creeps in slowly, with changing leaves of aspen and currants, or rushes in with blistering frosts occurring in August. Crabapples abound while berries become limited; and seeds are ripe for stripping. Fall reminds us that it's time to hunker down and prepare for the long cold winter.

Once again roots can be dug; they are best after a frost happens, sending all the sweet sugars downward. Hawthorn and mountain ash berries also become sweeter with the plummeting night temperatures.

Skunkbush berries ripen as summer gives way to autumn. Find some pink-lemonade-tasting berries lingering well into October.

Do not wait too long before visiting the scrub oaks: acorns are stowed away quickly by animals—surely, no one wants to miss out on an opportune harvest. Young chickweed and shepherd's purse can be found sprouting again for a last harvest of fresh greens.

Where to Find Fall Plants

Open Meadows, Disturbed Soils, or Forest Edges

alfalfa: seeds

amaranth: seeds

apple: fruit

black walnut: nuts

burdock: roots

chickweed: leaves, stems, flowers

chicory: roots

cow parsnip: seeds

crabapple: fruit

dandelion: roots

dock: seeds, roots

ground cherry: fruit

lamb's quarters: seeds

mallow: seedpods, roots

mountain parsley: roots

pepperweed: seedpods, roots

shepherd's purse: leaves

smooth sumac: fruit

strawberry blite: roots

sunflower: seeds

tumble mustard: seedpods

wild caraway: seeds

wild hops: strobiles

wild licorice: roots

yarrow: leaves

Desert, Among Sagebrush, or Rocky Soil

cota: leaves, stems, flowers

juniper: leaves, fruit

Mormon tea: stems

piñon: needles, nuts, resin

prickly pear: pads, fruit

scrub oak: nuts

skunkbush: fruit

Near Wetlands, Riverbanks, Lakesides, or Bogs

angelica: seeds, roots

bullberry: fruit

cattail: roots

cottonwood: bark, twigs

hackberry: fruit

stinging nettle: seeds

twisted stalk: fruit

watercress: leaves, seedpods

Woodlands or Partially Shaded Places

aspen: bark, twigs

chokecherry: bark, twigs, fruit, nuts

cleavers: seeds

Douglas fir: needles, resin

elderberry: fruit

fir: needles, resin

golden currant: fruit

gooseberry: fruit

hawthorn: fruit

hyssop: seeds

mountain ash: fruit

mountain gooseberry: fruit

northern bedstraw: seeds

pine: needles, resin, nuts

spruce: needles, resin

sweet root: roots

wax currant: fruit

wild grape: fruit

wild plum: fruit

wild rose: fruit

Wolf's currant: fruit

Winter

A quiet still descends. Blankets of snow cover the highlands, tucking the plants in against the long winter squall. In the midst of negative temperatures, we can turn to the evergreens for a winter's forage; they continue to provide us with their needles and resin. Even better would be the luck of finding a piñon cone with sweet nuts inside. Mormon tea can be gathered in the desert, and rosehips can be plucked throughout the land. All is not frozen in the mountain west.

Ripe juniper berries are the perfect forage for a snowy winter's day.

During this respite we can pull out our stash and indulge in the harvest of prior seasons, using our jams, cordials, and plant-infused oils, butters, and honey. Winter presents us with many opportunities to use the dried herbs of summer to blend teas and spices for nourishing our families. Add stored nutrient-dense herbs such as alfalfa leaves or the roots of dandelion and burdock to simmering broths.

Where to Find Winter Plants

Open Meadows, Disturbed Soils, or Forest Edges

amaranth: seeds

dock: seeds

Desert, Among Sagebrush, or Rocky Soil

juniper: leaves, fruit

Mormon tea: stems

piñon: needles, resin

Near Wetlands, Riverbanks, Lakesides, or Bogs

bullberry: fruit

cottonwood: buds, twigs

watercress: leaves

Woodlands or Partially Shaded Places

aspen: buds, twigs

mountain ash: fruit

wild rose: fruit

Douglas fir: needles, resin

pine: needles, resin

fir: needles, resin

spruce: needles, resin

Wild Edible Plants
of the Mountain West

A picturesque Colorado mountain stream with king's crown clinging to its rocky banks.

alfalfa

Medicago sativa

lucerne

EDIBLE leaves, flowers, seeds

Sprouted alfalfa seeds at the store can seem pricey—especially after you discover how easy it is to sprout your own crisp and fresh-tasting wild version at home.

How to Identify

A perennial herb of the pea family, alfalfa has the iconic clover pattern of leaves: each leaf is trifoliate, with three leaflets. The leaflets are oblong with tiny serrations around the apex, only slightly hairy on the underside and smooth on the top. Leaflets of sweet clover, a close look-alike before flowering, are serrated around the entire margin. Flowers grow in a clustered raceme, with many, usually purple flowers, but flower color can vary from white to light blue or a shade of purple. The seedpods are a tight coil shape and hold many tiny yellow-tan seeds.

Purple flowers of alfalfa are striking, but they also come in shades of blue and white.

Sprouting seeds

Any seeds can be sprouted for a living, wild food ingredient in the dead of winter. Store dormant seeds in a cool (under 70 degrees Fahrenheit) dark place with low humidity. When stored properly, seeds will stay active for about four years; you may prolong this by refrigerating or freezing your seeds, enabling you to store them for over a decade. Keep seeds that are high in oil, like sunflowers or pine nuts, stored in the freezer or refrigerator, as they can go rancid when stored in a warm place for too long.

To begin sprouting your seeds, take them out of storage and place them in a jar or bowl filled with water; a ratio of three parts water to one part seeds is optimum.

Soaking the seeds turns them from dormant into active seedlings. Always stir your seeds into the water to separate them, and make sure all seeds are surrounded by water. Soak your seeds for eight to 12 hours, straining off any floating seeds or debris from the water surface.

Drain and rinse the seeds very well, two or three times per day, after soaking. Make sure to drain seeds extremely well after each rinse; you don't want your seeds to be waterlogged. Let seeds breathe in between rinses. If storing in a container, let the container breathe; do not use a lid. Repeat the daily thorough rinses for three to five days, until your seeds have sprouted into the desired length.

Where and When to Gather

Find alfalfa growing in any kind of disturbed soil, whether it is pastureland or construction sites. Make sure where you are gathering is a clean spot, free of pollutants or heavy metals, as this plant pulls heavily from the soil. It prefers nutrient-rich soil. Alfalfa can be found in the foothills and mountains, flowering in summer. Gather young leaves in spring and early summer; seeds can be gathered in late summer or early fall.

How to Gather

Leaves are best while they are vibrantly green and young. Gather on a dry, sunny day if you intend to dry the plant for future use. Seeds need to be winnowed before being stored.

How to Eat

Alfalfa may not come with a taste that wows, but it is rich and earthy and chock-full of nutrients vital to our well-being. I like it raw or cooked; either way, it contains the full spectrum of B vitamins, along with A, D, and E. Flowers have a sweet, nutty taste and make a nice addition to salads along with the greens. I mix this fresh or dried herb in with broths, sauces, and soups. It is an easily disguisable nutrient-dense food that can even be chopped up and baked into muffins and egg dishes or scattered in mixed vegetables.

How to Preserve

Dry the leaves and flowers to store for tea blending or future culinary use. Seeds are edible only once sprouted and should then be touted as a superfood. The dried seeds can be sprouted for a tempting little green snack that can top sandwiches, salads, or soup in the middle of winter.

Future Harvests

No worries for the future when harvesting alfalfa: it is usually an escaped weed from the pasture.

Caution

Eat only sprouted seeds. Before consumption, talk to a healthcare practitioner or herbalist if you are pregnant or breastfeeding; if you are on heart medications, immunosuppressants, or photosensitizing drugs; or if you have had lupus or gout.
Be sure you have properly identified alfalfa before it blooms: its leaves resemble the young leaves of golden banner (*Thermopsis* species), a toxic plant with yellow flowers.

alpine sorrel

Oxyria digyna
mountain sorrel

EDIBLE leaves

Alpine sorrel is an edible plant for the adventurer's heart. It grows in mountainous terrain that most people aren't willing to climb. If you happen to love standing atop mountain peaks, then this tart, lemony-flavored little plant will be worth getting to know.

To distinguish alpine sorrel from other sorrels, look to find the pronounced indent of the kidney-shaped leaves where they meet the long petiole.

How to Identify

Alpine sorrel is a small plant found in the alpine tundra, with a basal rosette of kidney-shaped leaves. Leaves are long-stemmed, thick and fleshy, gaining hints of red with age. The stalk is long and greenish red with clusters of green flowers that will darken as they turn to seed. As the seedpod becomes winged, the outer edges turn a bright red.

Where and When to Gather

Find alpine sorrel high in the mountains, nestled between craggy rocks. It lives where not much other vegetation of the arctic tundra is found. It prefers to be near a water source, whether that is ephemeral spring snow runoff or the constant trickle of a mountain brook. Find alpine sorrel in late spring and summer.

How to Gather

Pluck off a few leaves from several different plants, spreading out your leaf harvest. The stalk, while in flower or seed, can be eaten as well. Gather only in areas where you can see a few dozen other plants.

How to Eat

While winding your way up a mountain path, be on the lookout for this dainty trailside nibble. The leaves are tart, like other sorrels, blending well into roughage or fruit salads. Macerate the leaves in a blender with a little sugar and warm water to make a tart and tangy summer beverage. Add wild mint, rose petals, or the berries of skunkbush or smooth sumac; strain and chill this wild beverage on ice. Leaves can also be cooked. Try them sautéed in garlic butter among other greens with fresh lemon squeezed on top.

How to Preserve

I've heard of alpine sorrel leaves and stems being pickled but have not tried this myself.

Future Harvests

Taking a few leaves here and there from plants will do no harm. Please do not uproot this native perennial. Leave the flowering stalks behind if there are not many other plants nearby.

Caution

Alpine sorrel contains oxalic acid. Do not eat large quantities if you are malnourished. When eaten raw, mixed among other foods, it should pose no risk to a healthy person. Boiling removes oxalates. People with kidney problems should avoid all foods that are high in oxalates.

amaranth

Amaranthus species

pigweed

EDIBLE leaves, seeds

Amaranth seeds are easy to collect and winnow for a backcountry morning porridge. All you need is a little water and some wild berries to sweeten their slightly bland, nutty flavor.

How to Identify

Amaranths can reach 6 feet tall or more, depending on the quality of soil in which they grow; plants of the mountain west tend to be shorter when growing in dry, compact, or rocky soil. Wide-based lanceolate or ovate leaves grow alternately up a green or red stalk. Green flowers are small, lack petals, and grow in a cone-like raceme. Seeds are smooth, shiny, and

The smaller, dark green leaves of amaranth can be used after the plant gets tall and flowers.

The sharp green bracts of the inflorescence will eventually hold an abundance of seeds. Gather the seeds once the bracts start to turn brown.

into a bucket, using your fingers to work them out. The seeds will then need to be winnowed, which releases the chaff from around the small seeds.

How to Eat

Use seeds whole, or grind them before placing them in a pot with twice the amount of water as seeds. Boil and reduce to a simmer, covered with a lid, for 20 minutes. Check your gruel often to ensure proper cooking, adding more water as needed. Some seeds will be drier than others, depending on when you harvest. The drier the seeds, the more water you will need. Cooked seeds blend well with lamb's quarters seeds and quinoa. Try combining ground seeds with various baking flours to enhance the nutritional value of breads, muffins, and crackers. Leaves can be used in place of kale or spinach; chop and add them to quiche, lasagna, or saag.

black, held in place by bristly brown bracts. The most common species in the mountain west are *Amaranthus retroflexus* and *A. powellii*.

How to Preserve

Amaranth seeds are wonderful to have on hand for a gluten-free breakfast gruel. Seeds can be roasted and ground for use in muesli or porridge. Stir in dried serviceberries, blueberries, strawberries, or raspberries stored from your summer forage or use a wild rose–infused honey for a sweetener.

Where and When to Gather

Head for a sunny spot. Gather young leaves in the spring or early summer, as older leaves are tougher and not always in the best shape later in the season. Seeds can be harvested in late summer, early fall, or even through the winter.

How to Gather

Pinch young leaves off the stalks. Make sure not to strip the entire plant of its foliage. Cut or break off the loaded seedheads of amaranth and beat the seeds off

Future Harvests

Amaranth is known to pop up just about anywhere the sun is shining and can be counted on to reseed itself year after year.

angelica

Angelica species
wild celery

EDIBLE stalks, seeds, roots

Once ground, the spicy-flavored seeds of angelica are ready for use in warming tea blends like chai.

How to Identify

First of all, be 110% certain with your identification of any and all plants in the carrot or parsley family (Apiaceae). This family contains some of the most toxic plants in North America: water hemlock (*Cicuta* species) and poison hemlock (*Conium maculatum*) can be fatal if ingested in even minuscule quantities, such as a seed or two (see caution).

Angelica has a showy umbel that resembles a firework, with many rounded clusters of white, light pink, or yellow flowers radiating from one point at the top of the stalk. Leaves are usually bipinnately divided into leaflets. The margins of the ovate leaflets are serrated. Leaf stems (petioles) have sheaths that hug the main stalk. Stems of angelica are a shade of purple or red and are always hollow. The

Angelica seeds can be gathered while green and dried for later use as an aromatic flavoring.

taproot is white or creamy and heavily scented, with a spicy celery aroma; most angelica roots are solid, whereas those of water hemlock and poison hemlock always have air pockets.

Where and When to Gather

Angelica prefers cool, moist mountain soil and can be found lining irrigation ditches or near riverbanks. Gather the leaves and stalks in summer. Seeds can be collected in late summer or fall. Roots can be harvested in spring or fall.

How to Gather

Gather the stalks and foliage of second-year plants, as they are more fragrant. Cut the tall stalk and strip leaves from the stem. Leaves can be dried and stored, while the stalk can be used fresh to make candies. Gather the seeds once they are fully ripened, and make sure to dry them thoroughly before storage. Roots can be dug, given a good washing, chopped, and dried using the lowest temperature in the oven or a dehydrator.

How to Eat

The chopped hollow stems of second-year plants are the most flavorful for being candied. Leaves, seeds, and stems can be infused in alcohol to make cordials and elixirs. Use roots, stems, leaves, or fresh seeds to make a simple syrup that can be used in cocktail blending or flavoring sodas.

Angelica leaflets are ovate and much wider than the thin lanceolate leaflets of water hemlock. Notice too that the primary veins of angelica end at the tips of the serrations of the leaflets.

The white umbel flowers of angelica can look very similar to those of water hemlock.

How to Preserve

Dried roots, leaves, and seeds can be stored individually in sealed containers, then used as culinary spices or blended into chai and other warming teas. Mix with herbs like hyssop, beebalm, and elder-flowers for a nice warm drink on a cool summer evening.

Future Harvests

Angelica grows abundantly throughout our region. If collecting seeds, leave at least one umbel in the stand full of seeds.

Caution

It's critical to differentiate angelica from water hemlock and poison hemlock. Angelica has ovate leaflets; water hemlock has lanceolate leaflets; poison hemlock has fern-shaped leaves (and a purple-spotted stem). Many botanists advise looking at the primary lateral leaf veins, too: if the veins end in between serrations, it is said to be one of the poisonous hemlocks; if the primary lateral veins end at the tip of the serration, "all is hip" (as they saying goes) and the plant is considered safe. I have seen variations to this with *Cicuta* species, however, so use this as only one of several identification tools.

The seeds of both angelica and water hemlock are ovate, but angelica's seeds are ribbed and winged (water hemlock seeds are only ribbed). The roots of water hemlock and poison hemlock, if cut longitudinally, will always show air pockets (something certain *Angelica* species sometimes show as well). Finally, angelica has an aromatic scent; however, if you have been digging the aromatic roots of angelica, any root will smell of it, and poison hemlock too has been noted to have a celery-like scent.

apple
Malus species
wild apple, feral apple

EDIBLE fruit

Stumble upon wild apple trees in the mountain west, and you've found a true treasure. The small fruits hold flavors that range from shockingly sweet to sharply bitter.

How to Identify

Wild apple trees can reach heights of 40 feet but are usually much smaller, hosting clusters of fragrant pink or white blooms every spring. Each flower is 1 to 2 inches wide and consists of five petals. The smooth bark is bronze or gray. Oval leaves grow alternately and have small serrations along the edges. Fruits can be big or small, though smaller varieties are usually called crabapples. Feral apples are at least 2 inches in diameter and range in color from yellow-green to orange and red.

Where and When to Gather

Apples linger around old homesteads and turn up around campgrounds and along roadsides and trails. Some could have been planted with intention; others may have sprouted up from tossed apple cores and fallen seeds. Find apple trees in fertile soils and among other trees in partial shade. This is not a tree you will find at high elevation: it grows mostly below 7,000 feet. Fruits begin to ripen in August and continue to produce until October, when the last fallen fruit can be found on the ground.

How to Gather

Many should be within reach—just pluck them from the tree. Sometimes you need a ladder or step stool to get the best-looking apples, but most of the time you can look to the ground and find ones the bugs haven't yet gotten to.

How to Eat

Wild apples will vary significantly in taste; even fruits from the same tree can taste different. Some are extremely astringent and bitter, while others are sweet, crisp, and juicy. Most wild apples are much better after they have been roasted, baked, or cooked into something sweet like pies. Apple slices also make a flavorful addition to kabobs for grilling.

If you happen to stumble upon an old apple grove, try sampling apples from each tree. Variance of tart, sour, and sweet apples is great for making cider, especially if you like your cider complex, with more notes of flavor.

Wild or feral apples are a real treat, especially if you find a tree that has sweet and not overly astringent fruit.

Find treasure troves of old apple groves in valleys filled with fertile soils.

How to Preserve

Wild apples have high amounts of pectin, more than the commercial varieties; this makes them a great addition to jellies or jams.

Apples can be sliced into thin pieces and placed in a dehydrator. Without one, lay slices out to air dry; in the arid west this takes several days. Flip the drying slices daily. Use of a dehydrator or oven set on a low temperature works well, and the slices are ready in hours as opposed to days. To keep them from browning, squeeze lemon or lime wedges over fresh slices before drying.

Use dried apples for tea, but first sprinkle them with spices like cinnamon, clove, and nutmeg for a warming winter beverage. Do this while they are wet with lemon juice.

Future Harvests

There are plenty to go around, but just a note, in case you fall in love with a particularly sweet-fruited tree: a sprouted apple seed does not represent the apple it came from. Apples do not come true from seed, meaning, there really is no telling what kind of apple tree will spring up if planted.

asparagus

Asparagus officinalis

shoots

It's worth seeking out this fabled wild food of the spring. Discover what all the fuss is about when you take a bite. Enjoy the crispness and a sweet flavor, richer than any store-bought asparagus—you may never go back.

How to Identify

It is best to find asparagus territory in the fall, when the plant looks nothing like the spring shoots. Look for the yellowed, branched plant, standing tall when all the other plants have died back. This perennial plant's woody stalk will be poking through snow, providing you with a perfect marker to the spot you should revisit once the snow melts in early spring. Shoots look just like their cultivated counterpart, although they may be a lot skinnier or sometimes giant. The tips are dark green when young, before the plant branches

Asparagus is delectable for a short window of only a few weeks before it becomes too tall and woody.

Find asparagus growing along fence lines that border ditches of flowing water.

out and forms small green flowers. Inedible red berries are produced by the mature female asparagus plant, making the many-branched green asparagus look like an ornate Christmas tree.

Where and When to Gather

Asparagus needs water to thrive, so start by looking there. It also doesn't grow well above 7,000 feet. Find tall, overgrown asparagus in midsummer when out fishing, or spot it growing in irrigated fields and ditches. Gather fresh young asparagus shoots in the springtime, as the temperatures warm.

How to Gather

Break off the stalk about 2 inches from the ground. The tender portions of the stalk should snap easily; if it seems tough, move higher up the stalk.

You will not see this year's asparagus right away, but you will spot last year's tall and branched dried plant stalks.

How to Eat

Wild asparagus is tastiest fresh: nibbling the crisp stalk is a spring delicacy that doesn't last. If stalks are young, tender, and thin, they need only a quick cooking or can be chopped up raw for salads. Thicker, older stalks may need to be peeled before eaten. I adore sautéed or baked wild asparagus in olive oil, with garlic, fresh Parmigiano-Reggiano, and a squeeze of lemon. It can be tossed on an open flame and charred or grilled as well.

How to Preserve

Pickled asparagus is a major hit in bloody marys or garnishing an antipasto plate. Frozen spears will remain fresh for up to a year; blanch them in boiling water for about two minutes, plunge them in an ice bath, dry, and freeze.

Future Harvests

Finding a thriving patch of asparagus is a springtime blessing. Keep it that way by picking from the same stalk once or twice in a season, as it will have a hard time growing and going to seed if overharvested. Always leave stalks behind to grow into strong mature plants, which will spread by rhizomes and possibly reseed.

Caution

The red berries of the female plant are toxic and should not be consumed.

aspen

Populus tremuloides

quaking aspen, trembling aspen

`EDIBLE` buds, bark, twigs

Create "from the forest" cocktail bitters from an extraction of wintertime buds, bark, and twigs.

How to Identify

People who move here from eastern North America often mistake aspen for birch, but unlike birch bark, aspen bark does not peel off spontaneously. Aspen trees are in the willow family (Salicaceae). Branches form

The beautiful bark of aspen holds the eyes of the forest. Resist the temptation to scar words into it, please.

slightly resinous buds in the winter that will turn into the quaking leaves and fuzzy catkins. Leaves are ovate to heart-shaped with serrated margins and a lighter-colored underside. They sit on a long flattened petiole, which is the reason leaves tremble, with a fluttering sound, in the slightest breeze. Aspen trees are 30 and 70 feet tall and grow in groves, each grove either male or female. The groves are one giant organism that is connected through the underground root system of the trees.

Where and When to Gather

Aspens are found in groves all over the mountain west, at elevations of 3,000 to 10,000 feet. Find them in mixed conifer forests, on sloping hillsides, and in mountain valleys. Gather the buds during the winter months. Bark is best gathered in the spring and fall when the tree is flowing with sap, making the outer bark easy to peel off the inner bark. The inner bark is what holds sweet and bitter properties.

How to Gather

Look to find wind-fallen branches or trees to harvest the buds from. The inner bark can be peeled off the recently fallen timber for making fresh extractions or drying for tea. Young twigs can be trimmed from trees while they host the buds. Strip buds off twigs, and use both twigs and buds in concoctions. Sample the sweet-tasting cambium of spring branches while peeling bark.

How to Eat

I like to nibble the winter buds for their pleasant vanilla, bitter-nutty taste; I will warn you though: it lingers. Infuse the buds along with young twigs and freshly peeled bark in brandy to create a unique bitters extraction. Blend in wild licorice root, rosehips, sweet clover, and cherry

Peeling bark

Bark peeling is easiest when the sap is running through the tree in spring. It makes separating the layers of dead outside bark and live inner bark more manageable. The live inside bark is what we are after for flavoring bitters or drying for tea. I like to use the flavors of aspen, cottonwood, and cherry barks.

I rarely take from live trees as it's so easy to find branches other ways. Find large wind-fallen branches or beaver-dropped trees, or contact a local tree trimmer with the specifics of the tree you would like to collect. Peel or scrape off the dry outer bark, and take a knife to slice long strips of the inner bark. Let bark strips dry thoroughly before storage. I don't even bother stripping the bark from small young twigs. I simply clip them into small pieces and toss them in with my peeled barks.

The thin, ovate or heart-shaped leaves of aspen tremble in the wind, setting off a round of applause in the woods.

bark for a "from the forest" bitters. Use this dashed into rum-, gin-, whisky-, and cognac-inspired cocktails. Add the simple syrups of spruce, pine, or fir for an especially woodsy drink.

How to Preserve

Dry peeled bark and store in a sealed container for blending teas in need of a bitter component. The white powder on the outside of the bark consists of a lot of natural yeast; it can be scraped off and has been used as a yeast starter.

Future Harvests

Never score around the entire circumference of any tree when gathering bark. It kills the tree and prevents the saps from coursing through the tree. If you must mark up a tree to try the bark or cambium, do so in a very small spot, or better yet, use only bark from the fallen branches you gather.

balsamroot

Balsamorhiza sagittata

arrowleaf balsamroot, Okanagan sunflower

EDIBLE leaves, stems, seeds, roots

The honey made from the roots of balsamroot will add a sweet piney-citrus, balsamic spice to your next cup of tea.

How to Identify

Flowers of balsamroot are bright yellow and form the characteristic Asteraceae formation: ray flowers radiating from the central disk flowers. Balsamroot leaves are a silvery green, and their undersides are even lighter in color. They stand out against the arid landscapes balsamroot likes to inhabit. The arrowhead-shaped leaves grow densely from the large taproot. Roots are thick, resinous, and corky-looking.

Where and When to Gather

Find balsamroot on rocky, dry, exposed hillsides at middle elevations, between 5,000 and 9,000 feet. It is best to gather the taproot before or while the plant is flowering. This is when the roots are most resinous and aromatic. Gathering after the plant dies back tends to yield a dried-up root that lacks many of the aromatics. Young spring leaves and stalks can be gathered when the plant begins to emerge, from spring to early summer. Gather seeds in late summer.

Balsamroot is one of the very first large yellow aster flowers to bloom each spring.

Leaves of balsamroot are arrowhead-shaped, soft, and grayish green.

How to Gather

Pick the choice young leaves and stems while they are small, soft, and pliable. To unearth balsamroot, try using a shovel, as a digging trowel may not be sufficient. Loosen the dirt around the root by digging in a circular rotation. Go for smaller plants, as they have more appetizing roots; bigger plants tend to have tough, dry roots.

How to Eat

Leaves and stems can be used in salads or cooked among other greens, imparting a sweet pine-like flavor. Try chewing on stems while hiking. I love making a honey out of the resinous root; it tastes spicy, with pine and balsamic-like flavors, and goes wonderfully in tea. The root can also be cooked and eaten. Cooking breaks down the root's inulin into sugars, which will render the root sweeter than when it's raw. The inulin converts slowly, though, so you do have to cook the root for a long time.

How to Preserve

The root can be chopped finely, dried, and stored in a sealed container. Seeds can be dried, roasted, and stored in a sealed container. Grind seeds to use in flour or porridge mixtures.

Future Harvests

If harvesting the root, you are taking life from the plant; therefore, harvest only when the hills are loaded with balsamroot. When gathering seeds, spread some down into the soil for future growth.

Caution

Balsamroot is in the Asteraceae, and some people may have allergic reactions to this plant family. Do not confuse balsamroot with *Arnica* species, which are inedible and will cause stomach irritation if ingested; arnica has heart-shaped, ovate, or lanceolate leaves.

beebalm

Monarda species

wild bergamot, oregano de la Sierra, mountain monarda

EDIBLE leaves, flower buds, flowers

The spicy oregano flavor of beebalm peaks in the summer's heat, while the flowers are vibrant and full of aroma.

How to Identify

Beebalm is a mint-family plant with a square stem and highly aromatic opposite leaves. Flowers radiate in clusters from the central seedhead and vary in color by species. Blooms of *Monarda fistulosa* are rose-pink or slightly purple; those of pony beebalm (*M. pectinata*) are sometimes white. The lanceolate leaves are slightly toothed and have a soft fuzzy feel from tiny hairs.

The opposite leaves of beebalm smell of lemony-oregano and can be used to bring spice and zest to dishes.

Infusing butter

Place a stick of butter in a bowl and let it soften to room temperature. Chop up herbs finely—as always, fresh is best. Use about 3 tablespoons of herbs, give or take, depending on how strong you want your butter to be. Mix together the herbs and butter. Place the herb butter on a piece of plastic wrap and roll the butter into a cylinder. Put the wrapped butter in the refrigerator for a day and unwrap for a nicely shaped stick of delicious herb-infused butter.

Another way is to gently heat the butter and herb together for 15 minutes. Cool and pour into a jar. Straining of the herb is not necessary.

My favorite herbs to infuse in butter are beebalm leaves, wild chive leaves, or rose petals. Cook anything and everything in these butters or simply slather them on baked goods.

Freeze the butter for long-term storage, as infused butter can mold within a few weeks.

Where and When to Gather

Beebalm is generally not found higher than 8,500 feet. It dwells in colonies, so you rarely see a single plant. It grows predominantly throughout the eastern foothills of the Rockies in sunny meadows and canyon bottoms, near dry or running creek beds. In early spring the young leaves can be gathered for culinary uses. In midsummer you will find the plants in full blossom and highly aromatic. The heat of the sun makes the aromatic oils more potent, making this the best time to gather.

How to Gather

Gather leaves and flowers from various plants or, if you are in a large enough stand, cut the top portion of the plant, which yields an ample amount of leaves and flowers.

How to Eat

Use the leaves of beebalm as you would fresh or dried oregano. Mexican and Italian dishes are excellent places to start when incorporating this herb. The flowers and buds hold even more spice and can be added to salads and salsas or dried for tea.

Use the flower and leaves to infuse honey, oils, butter, and vinegar. Infused honey can be drizzled over the top of fish before baking and used for a sweet and spicy flavoring in baked goods—or simply dollop some in your morning tea. Olive oil or vinegar infusions of beebalm jazz up a caprese salad with savory aromatics. Try slowly simmering the leaves and flowers in butter. This will leave you with another fabulous cooking ingredient to make modest meals such as scrambled eggs and toast wildly vibrant.

Use both the dried flowerheads and leaves when blending teas. Try beebalm along with yarrow leaves, wild mint, and elderflowers.

Beebalm is a choice tea when you are in the backcountry, as it doesn't need to be heated. It can easily be made with cold filtered creek water in a water bottle and sipped on while the herbs float around. Or try a sun tea infusion; simply set your drinking container in full sun for a few hours to infuse the flavor even further.

How to Preserve

Leaves have a taste similar to oregano with notes of lemon, which makes this a nice herb to add to the spice rack. Dry the leaves and store in an airtight jar to preserve the flavor. The flowers can be dried along with the leaves for teas.

Future Harvests

As with any native wildflower, be respectful of beebalm's habitat and encourage plants to thrive. Beebalm is easily propagated through cuttings, and the roots transplant well in the fall.

Caution

Should not be used in pregnancy.

bistort

Bistorta bistortoides

American bistort, smartweed, knotweed, smokeweed

EDIBLE leaves, flowers, roots

Roasted roots of bistort can be a nutty-tasting snack on their own or add a wild touch to a larger dish.

How to Identify

Bistort is in the buckwheat family (Polygonaceae). Flowers, mostly white but sometimes light pink, cluster together in a cylindrical spike. Bistort can be so common in alpine meadows that it can look like a soft blanket of snow in midsummer. It grows about a foot taller than most of the

Bistort has a long jointed stem with a cylindrical cluster of small white flowers.

other tundra plants, making it easy to spot. Most leaves are basal; only a few are carried on the jointed stalk. Leaves are elliptic, oblong, or lanceolate, and alternate.

Where and When to Gather

Bistort can be found blossoming in high alpine meadows, above treeline or below, in late summer. It prefers the moist climate created by clouds that linger over the mountains. Leaves can be gathered while the plant has enough growth to be identified and while it is in flower.

How to Gather

Gather the leaves by plucking a leaf or two from many different plants in order to spread out the harvest. Dig up the root when the plant nears the end of flowering.

How to Eat

The raw root, when nibbled on, is very astringent; however, cooking the roots brings out an almond-nutty flavor. Roasted roots are best of all. The roasted and chopped roots go well in stir-fries. Use the tender young leaves fresh, in salads; sprinkle flowers on top.

Future Harvests

Forage with care, especially when taking roots of bistort. Spread out your harvest through a large area.

black walnut

Juglans nigra
eastern black walnut

EDIBLE green hulls, nuts

Don't try to use a nutcracker on the hard exterior shell of black walnuts: it will surely break or be ineffectual. To extract the rich-tasting walnut's nutmeat, use your primitive skills and smack the shells open with a rock or hammer.

How to Identify

Black walnut trees have fairly straight trunks with deeply furrowed bark. Color of bark varies from light to dark gray. Alternate leaves are composed of 15 to 23 leaflets that are pinnately divided, with a single leaflet at the end. The male flowers are long green catkins that droop from the branches in spring. Female flowers form in clusters of two to five at the end of branches. The female flowers are what turn into the round green fruits. Leaves and the green hulls of the fruit are highly aromatic and smell of citrus with a hint of pine. In

Round green hulls of black walnuts have a pleasant pine-citrus fragrance.

Cracking black walnuts open can be quite the task. Try to strike the shell on a side that is not the seam.

autumn, when the fruits ripen, the hull will soften and turn to a yellow-brown, then finally go black.

Where and When to Gather

Although not native to the mountain west, black walnut is definitely a commonly found tree in cities of lower elevation. Find black walnut trees in fertile soils of farmlands, or neighborhood yards below 6,000 feet. Gather the young green hulls in midsummer, while they are soft enough to cut into quarters. Black walnuts can be gathered for nutmeat in fall, when the hulls have started to brown.

How to Gather

Young green hulls can be plucked from trees. It's usually the case that you'll need to ask permission, because the tree is in someone's yard. I have had only positive responses of "What is that tree? It makes a huge mess! Take as much as you'd like."

Pick up the freshly fallen, browned hulls in the fall. Wear gloves if you want to keep your hands from turning black. Peel away the outer hulls the day you gather, when they are easiest to pry apart. After husking away the hulls, rinse your black walnut shells well. Then allow them to air dry for a few days in a mesh bag, or spread out on a table, rotating them daily.

To crack the nuts, I put the whole walnut into a paper bag and lightly hit it with a hammer. This way shrapnel does not fly at your face and all the walnut is contained in the paper bag. Place the walnut on its side, and strike the nut opposite to any seams, which better exposes the nutmeat. Cracking it open on the seam makes the nutmeat harder to extract.

How to Eat

Young green walnuts make nocino, an Italian bitter cordial with spicy sweet citrusy tones. Start by infusing vodka with the quartered hulls, lemon zest, cloves, vanilla, and cinnamon. Let this infuse for four to six weeks and strain. After straining, sweeten your nocino with simple syrup, honey, or maple syrup.

Nuts can be eaten raw and used anywhere an English walnut would be used. Use nuts to top brownies, toss into salads, or blend into pestos and nut butters. Nuts can also be roasted once out of the shell.

How to Preserve

After the hulls are removed, black walnuts can be stored over winter while still in the shell. Store in the freezer or a cool, dry location.

Future Harvests

Harvest with impunity (and, if necessary, permission): the decaying nutshells litter sidewalks and turn them black in the fall, making it quite okay to take bucket-loads of nuts.

Notice the pinnately compound leaflets of black walnut are not directly opposite one another.

bluebells

Mertensia species
mountain bluebells, chiming bells

EDIBLE leaves, flowers

Bluebells lure you in with the iridescent, oceanic shimmer of their blue-pink tubular flowers. Leaves, with the faint richness of an oyster mushroom, take you seaside with their flavor.

How to Identify

A variety of bluebells are commonly found throughout the mountain west. Plants can be dwarfed in size and scattered through mountain meadows or quite tall and growing in large bountiful stands. Leaves are ovate to lanceolate, and are either hairy or smooth. They can be noticeably veined and grow alternately up the flowering stalk. Nodding light pink, purple, or blue tubular flowers blossom in branched clusters.

Where and When to Gather

Bluebells adorn the edges of forest floors, mountain meadows, and alpine streams,

Dwarf bluebells (*Mertensia brevistyla*) has little hairs on the leaves, which are therefore best either finely minced or cooked. Gather leaves and flowers in late spring and early summer.

Tall bluebells (*Mertensia ciliata*) has large, hairless leaves with an oyster mushroom flavor.

soaking up the spring moisture from rain showers and snowmelt runoffs. Gather the leaves and flowers from spring to summer when they are young and vibrant.

How to Gather
Many blooming bluebells can be found spread through fields, or in tall stands. This makes it easy to pluck a few leaves and flowers from many plants, not just one.

How to Eat
Enjoy the leaves and flowers in salads or on top of sandwiches raw. Chop up or use sparingly, as some species' leaves can be hairy and unpalatable in large amounts raw. To me, bluebells either taste like an oyster mushroom or have a full-bodied nutty flavor. The dense leaves have a succulent texture, making them a choice

leaf for cooking. Leaves hold up well in stir-fries, soup, and egg scrambles and also add an earthy-green flavor sure to remind you of the mountain meadows.

Future Harvests
Although abundant where they grow, graze these native plants with care. There is no need to uproot the plant, or cut down a whole stand. Pick a few leaves and flowers from each plant.

Caution
Eating large quantities (a few cups) of *Mertensia* species can reportedly cause gastric upset; bluebells contain small amounts of alkaloids, but adding leaves to spring salads and eating minimal amounts should have no health implications.

blueberry

Vaccinium species
huckleberry, whortleberry, bilberry

EDIBLE fruit

Vaccinium fruits travel under different common names as they cross the continent—huckleberry, bilberry, whortleberry, or simply the blueberry—and the size and color of the berries varies by region as well. But all are absolutely worth seeking out for their remarkable flavor, some with hints of vanilla.

How to Identify

These shrubs can be tiny, standing not more than a few feet from the ground and usually sprawling along a hillside or sparse forest. Leaves grow alternately along a woody stem. The flowers, shaped like a bell, are usually whitish pink, and they have an inferior ovary that swells into purple, red, or blue berries. At the tip of the berries is a star-like mark from the sepal, where the flower once was.

Some blueberries, like *Vaccinium myrtillus* var. *oreophilum*, are very tiny, but size doesn't matter when it comes to flavor.

Where and When to Gather

Berries begin to ripen in July, depending on your elevation and location. Harvesting can last until late August. Vacciniums like to grow in acidic soils, so you will find them in or near conifer forests. Blueberries can feel elusive in some parts of the mountain west. Usually this is because you have not visited the right place or you forgot to look low enough. Blueberries can be found in Colorado, Wyoming, western Utah, and (rarely) Nevada. They are primarily found in the Pacific Northwest, Alberta, Idaho, and western Montana. Montana even has a huckleberry industry, with their milkshakes and preserves.

How to Gather

Down on hands and knees may be the easiest way to get acquainted with blueberries. When the shrubs are loaded with ripe berries, you can sweep your hand

At first glance you may see no berries at all, until you get down on your hands and knees to scavenge.

through the plant and comb out the fruits. The berries may be abundant and you would not even know it.

How to Eat

It is hard to keep a good quantity, because they are so delicious! Vacciniums have a taste all their own, only slightly comparable to commercial blueberries. Enjoy straight off the plant or with a dusting of sugar. Not only are they the best-tasting blueberries, but a hint of vanilla may even be in there. What can't this tiny fruit be whipped into? Making a to-do list of all the possibilities would be a daunting proposition. A must-try is either a blueberry crisp or pie.

How to Preserve

Freezing blueberries is a great way to enjoy them all year long in smoothies. Mashed berries can be added to vodka for a wild infusion to add to cocktails. Berries can be simmered and transformed into jams, fruit leathers, and simple syrups.

Future Harvests

Be conscious of the fact that many critters, big and small, rely on berries for food. I am sure blueberry is a favorite with bears and grouse. Enjoy what you like, but leave some berries behind.

blue mustard

Chorispora tenella
musk mustard, crossflower

EDIBLE leaves, stalks, flowers, seedpods

Blue mustard is one of the first mustard greens to pop up in early spring, providing us with a soft spicy flavor that helps awaken us from our winter-foraging slumber.

How to Identify

In early spring you can first identify the basal leaves that are oblong-lanceolate and slightly toothed. The leaves are steely blue-green and grow alternately along the branched stalks. Soon the plant blooms, carpeting the ground with soft lavender. The four petals of blue mustard sit atop a long tubular calyx and are arranged in the typical mustard-family cross-shaped pattern. Edges of the pinkish purple petals are wavy and pinched in at the base. The somewhat flattened seeds are contained in a cylindrical silique that curves upward into a slender beak.

A full plate of salad greens is here, just waiting to be picked and drizzled with herb-infused oil and balsamic vinegar.

Some of the first leaves are lobed or toothed, but as the flowering stalk emerges, leaves become lanceolate.

Where and When to Gather

Find this adventive small mustard in disturbed soils throughout most of the mountain west. It does very well in poor soils, taking up swaths of real estate where not many plants could grow. Gather from early spring, ending with the seedpods in summer.

How to Gather

Pinch or cut at the base of this plant's basal leaves. While the plant is young and vibrant, pick fresh green leaves from its base and along the stalk. Save the stalk as well, if it is still tender. Flower racemes and seedpods can be plucked off.

How to Eat

Older leaves and seedpods are spicier than the younger leaves, which are milder with the first notes tasting of sweet mushrooms and the end bite being slightly mustardy. The whole plant has a musky odor that some may find unpleasant, but it blends well when combined with other mustard greens in a wild salad bowl. Use leaves, flowers, chopped young stalks, and seedpods in pestos and salsas as well.

Future Harvests

Do not feel bad about harvesting or even uprooting this pesky weed. It is probably better that you do so, as blue mustard spreads like crazy from seed, quickly taking over entire yards, boulevards, or city blocks.

Brandegee's onion

Allium brandegeei

EDIBLE leaves, flowers, bulbs

In spring just after the snow has melted, while walking in the high alpine, I smell this little onion's potently aromatic flowers long before I find it in my path. The whole plant tastes strongly of onion.

How to Identify

Pinch a leaf of Brandegee's onion. If it smells like an onion, it probably is one. This particular wild onion is a tiny plant, low to the ground, with thin, flat, chive-like leaves that are not hollow. Its small, white (and sometimes pink-striped) flowers are held in clusters that bloom near the base of the narrow leaves. The bulbs are round; they can be deep for such a little plant but are worth a gentle dig.

Look low to the ground for this little onion; it prefers sunny slopes.

Where and When to Gather

Brandegee's onion usually grows in vast colonies in the sandy and rocky soils of the mountain west. It springs up shortly after the snow has melted, anytime from April through July, and grows at 4,000 to 10,000 feet in elevation. There are many species of wild onion to be found in the Rockies. Brandegee's onion just happens to be my local favorite.

How to Gather

The flowers are easy to pluck, as are the leaves. If you want to take the whole plant, carefully dig lightly and deep to find the bulb; it is small but so worth it.

How to Eat

The leaves and flowers are delightful in a salad or tossed on top of any dish, really. They not only add beauty but a spiced flavor that can make the blandest greens taste exciting. The bulb can be used just as a traditional onion would be; add it to stir-fries, soups, sauces, and stews. Add the whole plant to salsas and pestos, or blend with sour cream for a wild French onion dip.

How to Preserve

The bulbs can be pickled or canned in any way imaginable. The leaves and flowers make fantastic infused vinegar or oil and

These small bulbs are the perfect size for a cocktail onion.

The entire plant can be minced and used raw or cooked for a pungent onion flavor.

can be added to homemade salad dressings. Brandegee's onions are nice to have
preserved or dried for future combinations
with other wild foods.

Future Harvests

Be mindful to leave a few flowers behind,
and do not take all the foliage from one
plant. This should be easy, because these
onions tend to grow close together and in
bunches. If you are using the whole plant,
be careful not to take too many from one
single patch; spread out the harvest to keep
the colony hardy.

Caution

The young leaves of death camas (*Toxicoscordion venenosum*) and mountain death
camas (*Anticlea elegans*) could be mistaken for *Allium* species. Be certain with
your identification and do not rely solely
on smell, as the onion scent will linger on
your fingers and a non-scented root can
seem to smell of onion. Roots of the
aforementioned toxic plants are oval with
black scales.

bullberry

Shepherdia argentea
silver buffaloberry

EDIBLE fruit

Wait until the weather turns and the first frost occurs to harvest tart-astringent bullberries, with their faint taste of chokecherry.

How to Identify

Bullberry is a thorn-ridden shrub-like tree with glossy, scaly-looking leaves. Scale spots on both sides of the leaves have a silver or bronze color. The dense, leathery leaves grow opposite and are oblong-lanceolate in shape. Thorns can be over an inch long and very sharp. Bark is silver-gray in color; the old growth bark peels off in long strips. New growth at the ends of branches has a mealy white coating. Berries are spotted with silver scales, similar to that of the leaves. They are orange, turning red when ripe. Canadian buffaloberry (*Shepherdia canadensis*), a shrub with no thorns, grows in similar regions; its berries are a little more astringently bitter but can be used interchangeably.

Gathering bullberries by hand can be tough, as plants come with thorns that can reach to at least an inch long. Laying a blanket down under the tree and shaking the fruit down will help make your experience a little less painful.

Find bullberry as a shrubby tree.

Where and When to Gather

Find bullberry thickets close to rivers, among cottonwood trees and willows; also find it growing in alkaline soils and on grassy hillsides. Canadian buffaloberry can be found in arid sagebrush country or basking in the sun on canyon edges. For the finest-tasting fruit, it is best to do the gathering in the late fall or winter, after the berries have endured a few good frosts. The frost helps to sweeten the berries.

How to Gather

Mind the thorns! To gather bullberries, lay a blanket or tarp on the ground, under the branches, and find a thornless place to grab and shake the tree. You can also use a stick to gently knock the berries loose from the branches. Collect the fallen fruit.

How to Eat

If you want to use them in jellies, jams, or marmalades, pick bullberries before the first season's frost. The berries are juicy and more full of pectin then. Berries also make a nice rendition of a cranberry sauce; use them in combination with other fruits if you find them to be too tart. Simply cooking and adding sugar does them just fine, but try adding blood oranges along with some traditional cranberries to smooth out the flavor.

Spiced sauces and glazes for wild game like buffalo, elk, and mule deer can be

Canadian buffaloberries (*Shepherdia canadensis*) have wider, darker green leaves and grow on a bush that is without thorns.

made by cooking down the berries with cinnamon, clove, nutmeg, and other spices, or flavor boosters like vanilla and honey. Thanks to the presence of saponins, berries can also be mixed with equal parts water and plenty of sugar, and whipped into a frothy meringue.

How to Preserve

Dry berries and store for later use in trail mixes or baked goods. Fruit leathers can be made by mashing and cooking down the berries with a little water. Or, following Native American tradition, mash the raw berries into formed patties and let them dry in the sun; flip patties daily to prevent molding.

Future Harvests

Gathering the berries of Canadian buffaloberry or bullberry will not harm plants; just be careful not to get stuck on the long thorns of bullberry.

Caution

Bullberries contain saponins, which give them their bitter flavor and frothiness. Saponins are not harmful to the body and are broken down through cooking. Eat *Shepherdia* species in small quantities and avoid them if irritation occurs.

burdock

Arctium species

gobō

EDIBLE shoots, leaves, stalks, roots

Burdock is a versatile player in the forager's kitchen: its sweet, subtle flavor and meaty firm consistency lend themselves well to cooking, pickling, and grating raw.

How to Identify

Big, soft basal leaves mark the first year of this hardy biennial. Leaves are bright green on top, lighter in color on the underside, and are covered in velvety fuzz. The basal rosette of leaves can grow to about 18 inches across. Second-year plants send up large leafy flowering stalks. The thistle-ish flowers are a magenta puff of disc florets surrounded by spiky green bracts. These hooked bracts are what turn into the brown clinging burred seedpods, which host a few hundred seeds each. Burdock roots grow deep, averaging depths of

A comparison could be drawn between burdock leaves and an elephant's ears.

Be careful of your clothes when you walk past burdock, as its seedpods will stick and stay like Velcro.

around 2 feet; brown outer flesh, which can hold a lot of dirt, covers the dense creamy white interior.

Where and When to Gather

Burdock can be found throughout the mountain west, mostly growing where humans have settled, near ranches, farms, or old homesteads. Being a lover of disturbed soils, this biennial can also frequent places where soil is not so compacted, such as a tilled garden or worked-over farmland. Roots should be gathered in the fall of the first year or while the plant has only basal leaves the following spring. Shoots and young leaves can be gathered in early spring. Roots and stalks are more tender before the plant flowers; after blooming, both become somewhat woody and not very palatable.

How to Gather

The taproot of burdock can grow enormously deep. I have to admit, I am rarely able to get the entire root out of the ground when harvesting. I like to grow burdock in the garden, which gives me the advantage of prepping the soil, keeping it sort of loose, so the root will be easier to harvest come fall. If the brown outer flesh of the root is caked with too much dirt, simply peel it off after a good rinse. Young leaves and shoots of first-year plants can be eaten as well and should not be tossed aside when harvesting the root.

How to Eat

Burdock root is a staple in my bone broth recipes as well as a "secret" ingredient in my soups, stews, stir-fries, and mashed potatoes. Its sweet flavor and firm, crisp bite hold up well in recipes that require extended cooking. Burdock browns easily when being processed. Keep a bowl of vinegar water on hand; dipping sliced pieces into the vinegar water will help preserve the root's white color if you are using it raw in salads.

The thick stalks of second-year plants can be peeled and boiled until tender. Shoots and young leaves can be cooked along with other vegetables for an extra boost of iron, magnesium, and calcium.

How to Preserve

Burdock root can be chopped up fresh and dehydrated for easy use in the kitchen during the winter months. Increase its richness by roasting the minced root in the oven or an iron skillet. Roasted burdock roots combine nicely with other roasted wild roots, such as dandelion and chicory. Store dried root in a glass jar for use in teas or broths.

Fresh burdock, dandelion, and dock roots can be combined to create a mineral- and nutrient-packed vinegar extraction (see sidebar on page 239). Use this as the base for dressings or marinades. Try pureeing the infused vinegar with carrot, ginger, and beebalm for a superb salad dressing.

Decoct the roots in boiling water for 10 to 15 minutes and strain; make sure to add a dollop of acorn butter before sipping. Burdock roots can be sliced into long slender pieces and pickled with wine, rice, or sherry vinegar and salt.

Future Harvests

There is little to no concern in harvesting *Arctium* species in the mountain west. In some places burdock is not so common, but growing it in the garden is quite easy: taking seeds from a plant and spreading them in tilled soil should do the trick.

Caution

Steer clear if you have a known allergy to sunflower family (Asteraceae) plants. An allergy may show as itchiness or stomach irritation.

cattail

Typha species

`EDIBLE` shoots, flower spikes, pollen, roots

Cattails are a food of many seasons, for many reasons. Taste the fresh spring shoots with their cucumber flavor, enjoy nibbling cooked flower spikes like corn on the cob, and take home the golden treasure of the pollen, which transforms and enriches any flour blend.

How to Identify

In midsummer look for the long, round, slender stalks of broadleaf cattail (*Typha latifolia*) or narrowleaf cattail (*T. angustifolia*) rising up from marshy ground, with a wavery brown flower spike waiting to turn to seed fluff. Cattails have long, flat, lanceolate basal leaves that stand tall along the stalk, which itself can grow as high as 10 feet. Cattail leaves have chambered air pockets. Both male and female flower spikes are carried at the top of the stalk. The topmost, male flower spike produces pollen that fertilizes the lower, female spike, the one that eventually turns to fluffy seed.

Where and When to Gather

Cattails are mostly found at lower elevations in standing water and riparian areas. Find them along irrigation ditches, marshes, and river inlets that receive full sun. Plants can be foraged in three seasons of the year. Young shoots should be gathered in early spring, as soon as the water has thawed and the green leaves are getting long, before the plant flowers. The young flower spikes should be gathered while green; leave some behind so you can come back to harvest the pollen in early summer. Harvesting the inner core can be done until about midsummer. Roots and lateral rhizomes can be gathered in fall or early spring.

How to Gather

Cut off the aerial portions of the plant, stripping the leaves to reveal the white inner core of young shoots. The young flower spikes of the female and male portion of the plant are edible and quite tasty while still green and hidden within the leaves of the stalk. Find the cylindrical protrusion of the spikes and shuck away the leaves, as you would corn, to reveal the edible miniature cobs. They can also be eaten once exposed from the central stalk, but hurry and catch them before they start to brown.

Gather cattail pollen by bending the male spike into a paper bag or into a bucket.

It can be quite the task to locate the roots and cut them free in the water. Digging with your hands around the base of the cattail, you will feel the lateral rhizomes. Younger ones are edible. Mature

Cattail's young green flower spikes are best before or just after they emerge from the inner leaves of the stalk. Shuck off the leaves and boil or roast like mini cobs of corn.

The golden pollen of cattail can be shaken into a bucket or paper bag. Attempt this harvest maneuver on a non-windy day, or all the pollen will blow away.

rhizomes are fibrous and too tough to eat but can be processed for their starch. Once you get them home, give them a good scrubbing to remove debris. Then pound them out in a pail of water, really working them and scrubbing to release the starch. The starch will float to the bottom after a rest of several hours. Decant off the water and store the liquid starch in a jar that can be frozen for later use or dehydrated. After drying the starch out, grind it into a fine powder and store for use as a thickening agent.

How to Eat

Young shoots have a bite comparable to hearts of palm with a bamboo shoot–like flavor. Use them in Asian stir-fries, steam alone for a side dish, or eat them raw, tossed decoratively onto salads. For a quick, raw dish of a cattail's inner core, which has a mild cucumber flavor, simply slice the shoot, dust with wild chive–spiced salt, and drizzle with beebalm-infused olive oil.

The green flower spikes can be boiled or roasted until tender then slathered in salted butter and eaten down to the stalk, like a mini corn on the cob.

Young rhizomes can be chopped and eaten raw or cooked. The starch from mature rhizomes can be utilized in either its liquid or dried form to thicken soups, stews, or gravies.

How to Preserve

Store pollen in the freezer for maximum freshness. Add pollen to smoothies or mashed potatoes to enrich them with protein. Pollen can also be substituted for some portion of other flour(s) to make any recipe more hearty; start by switching in a quarter-cup of pollen, until you figure out the consistency that works best.

Future Harvests

Gather cattails only at lower elevations, where they grow most abundantly. Finding them above 9,000 feet is rare in most parts of the mountain west. Scatter the seedy fluff of the female flower throughout the marshland to help establish a better population.

Caution

Cattails will grow happily in contaminated waters, so be very careful about where you are harvesting them. Also, in spring before the cattails have flowered, their leaves resemble those of irises, which should not be consumed. Iris leaves are veined, and iris stalks have a flattened oval shape. Cattail leaves are not veined, and stalks are round.

chickweed

Stellaria media

EDIBLE leaves, stems, flowers

Chickweed is easy to pull or pinch from the ground by the handful and can be used in place of sprouts on sandwiches or pho.

How to Identify

Chickweed is a voracious little weed chock-full of nutrients. It has small white flowers and opposite succulent leaves, but the line of fine hairs along the central stem is what distinguishes chickweed from other similar-looking plants. Plants trail low, their stems forming branched mats and rooting back to the ground. Flowers, singly or in a small cluster, adorn the tip of each stem. At first glance, flowers may look like they have 10 petals, but there are only five—each petal just has a very deep indentation.

Where and When to Gather

Chickweed prefers a cool climate, particularly flourishing in spring and sometimes fall, which keeps it vibrant and crisp for harvesting. Find it growing in the shaded corner of yards, disturbed soils, and sheltered semi-moist areas. Come the heat of the summer, it can wither or become dry and stout. This little weed is harvestable

A single line of fine white hairs runs up the stems of chickweed.

The five white petals of chickweed are shaped like very deeply lobed hearts.

almost all year long. It seems to just keep growing, providing new shoots in late fall and possibly in the winter under conifers or if the snow on a south-facing aspect is melted. Chickweed is best gathered just before or right as it flowers, as the plant dies back after flowering.

How to Gather

This plant will rarely be found alone. It grows in patches, making it easy to harvest. The whole plant is edible. Try to snap off only the top few inches. It is okay if you accidentally pull up the whole plant; it's easy to do. Rinse your harvest well, removing any dirt, and lay it on a towel. Roll the damp chickweed up in the towel and place it in the refrigerator for a few days to a week.

How to Eat

Raw chickweed is ideal for many purposes. Stems, leaves, and flowers are a package deal that can be juiced into a green slurry like wheatgrass, using a masticating juicer. Gather a handful for a sandwich garnish or as an excellent green addition to your smoothie. Add to pesto and other spreads or use in place of bean sprouts in fresh Vietnamese spring rolls.

How to Preserve

The whole plant can be infused into vinegars for the extraction of its minerals and vitamins. Chickweed can be kept in the fridge for up to a week or so, depending on the juiciness of the stems. The whole stem can also be thrown in the freezer for months and pulled out, bright green and tasting fresh. Juiced or pureed chickweed can be poured into ice cube trays and frozen for later use in smoothies.

Future Harvests

Overharvesting chickweed can be hard to do since it sows itself so well. Do be careful if you fall in love and want to nurture it in your garden; it can drastically take over.

chicory

Cichorium intybus

succory

leaves, flowers, roots

Chicory is a popular root that is roasted and ground for its coffee-like flavor—it's even made it into commercial coffee blends out of New Orleans.

How to Identify

The blue flowers of chicory can be seen dotting the shoulders of dirt roads and highways all over the mountain west. Each flower blooms for only one day. When any part of the plant is broken, it exudes milky sap. Young basal leaves look similar to dandelion leaves; however, the jagged leaf edges of chicory point both outward and upward, not toward the leaf base like those of dandelions do. Young leaves could also be confused with another edible plant, wild lettuce; however, chicory lacks the prickles on the underside of the central leaf vein. Chicory can reach heights of 5 feet and has a scraggly look with its somewhat woody, jointed stem. Leaves and flowers grow sporadically along the branched stems.

Spot the periwinkle-colored flowers of chicory growing along roadsides in late summer.

Chicory petals can be plucked off and dashed over summer plates for a color that reflects the sky.

Where and When to Gather

Chicory grows abundantly in some places and is rarely seen in other areas of the west. It likes to grow below 7,500 feet and is usually found in the lowlands between mountain ranges, along roadsides or in sunny pastures. In springtime, chicory provides a crop of bitter young greens that rival escarole or endive (*Cichorium endivia*), its cultivated cousins.

How to Gather

Gather spring leaves while they are young and growing as a rosette. Roots are impressively large and take some digging to uncover; they are best harvested after the plant turns brown. Root crowns can be saved and used as miniature endive. Gather flowers for their petals only, as the green bract can be too bitter.

How to Eat

Chicory leaves, while young and tender, are the perfect bitter green to enliven any salad. The root crowns are fantastic sautéed in garlic and oil, tasting like mini escarole. Blue flower petals can be picked off the bract and used to decorate salads or entrees.

How to Preserve

Dried and roasted roots of chicory have a long shelf life if stored in a sealed container. Chop roots finely before roasting to ensure the longevity of your coffee grinder blades. Grind roasted roots as you would coffee beans, and brew your tea using a French press for best results.

Future Harvests

Chicory reseeds itself quite well, which is why you can find this nonnative plant on noxious weed lists. Feel free to harvest roots at your will.

Caution

Chicory is in the Asteraceae, and some people may have allergic reactions to this plant family.

chokecherry

Prunus virginiana

bird cherry

EDIBLE bark, twigs, flowers, fruit, nuts

One of the most abundant fruit trees of the mountain west happens to bear the smallest fruit, each packed with an intense sour-cherry bite.

How to Identify

Chokecherry trees are very abundant in the mountain west along rivers and highways and in subalpine forests. If it is late spring, identifying can be easy. Look for shrubby trees with long white clustered racemes of flowers that hang from the sides of the branches. Find a good group of trees in flower, and return to this prime spot to harvest cherries later in the summer. Thin-trunked trees grow from a few feet to 10 feet tall; they tend to be heartier in the foothills and smaller and more shrub-like the higher in elevation they grow. Leaves are shiny green with a lighter hue on the underside; they are oval with little jagged edges and arranged alternately along the stem. Bark ranges from gray to reddish brown, with horizontal lighter-colored air pores called lenticels. Fruit is a drupe, a berry with only one seed—the nut or pit, in chokecherry's case. Berries ripen to an almost black color late in the summer.

Where and When to Gather

Trees are found near streams, along ditches, in canyons and conifer forests. Gather the flowers in spring when they are highly aromatic. Beat the birds to the fruits when they are about a quarter-inch in size and darkened to black, in late summer or early fall.

How to Gather

Handpicking cherries can be time-consuming. Snipping off the twig that the drupes hang on is a faster method of removing them from the tree; for use in larger batches, freeze the whole stem of cherries to make picking the cherries off the stems easier. Trim the flower spikes off branches with pruners.

How to Eat

Flowers can be harvested for infusing into honey or making liquor cordials. The tips of the chokecherry twigs give a bitter flavor, while the blossoms hold nice almond-cherry aromatics, making this a great herb for cocktail bitters as well.

The fruits will vary in flavor from tree to tree. Taste a few cherries before you take a whole bunch from one tree. Some are very tart and astringent—the flavor that makes your mouth pucker and muscles twinge. Others have more of a sweet-and-sour

Harvest chokecherries once they have darkened to black, but hurry before the birds eat them all!

Fragrant white flowers light up riverbanks and streets in spring. Use flowers to infuse alcohol or to make a simple syrup.

taste. It can be best to pick cherries from several different shrubs for a superb taste combination. Use cherries to make dessert fillings and ice cream. Add sugar or a sweetener to cut the tartness.

The nuts of chokecherry are high in prussic acid, a form of cyanide, but crushing them and exposing them to oxygen or cooking them renders the nuts safe to eat.

Use a food mill to remove the pits and make fruit leathers. Or use the whole fruit and mash into a pulp. The crushed nut has an almond flavor that pairs nicely with the tart cherries. Do be careful of the shells; they have been known to crack teeth. Fruit leathers can be made this way raw or cooked.

How to Preserve

Try freezing whole cherries or cherry mash for future use. Liquors, syrups, wine, and jam or jellies can be made to preserve the cherries into winter. Berries can be dehydrated or dried whole and then stored. Chew the fruit off the nut, or if you wait long enough, it seems the nut gets soft enough to crunch up along with the skin. Twigs and the bark of the branches can be peeled and dried for use in teas.

Future Harvests

Forage away—the next generation of this common tree is assured.

cleavers

Galium species

goosegrass, bedstraw

EDIBLE leaves, stems, seeds

Cleavers have a subtle sweet flavor and are loaded with vitamin C, lending themselves well to springtime smoothies and pestos.

How to Identify

Cleavers are most recognized by the whorled leaf pattern that runs up the square stem. The leaves grow in whorls of six to eight and are oblanceolate in shape. Stems are leggy and branched; they sprawl across the ground rather than standing straight up. Both leaves and stems have tiny hooked hairs, by which means the plant is able to creep over other plants.

Flowers are tiny, white, yellow, or green in color, with four petals, and blossom in late spring. Cleavers has fuzzy, sticky burrs or seedpods that easily stick to socks and shoelaces.

Where and When to Gather

The tender young leaves of cleavers can be gathered from spring until midsummer. Find vibrant green cleavers on montane

With their whorled leaf pattern and sticky burrs, cleavers are a cinch to identify.

Toss a handful of fresh cleavers greens into your next smoothie, or roast the dried seeds for a coffee-flavored tea.

How to Eat

Cleavers is not the best plant to eat raw, as it has a rough, semi-unpleasant texture that can make your throat itchy. I prefer to use it in smoothies and green drinks, or macerated into pestos and dips. Cleavers has a sweet vanilla-like flavor while it is still young. Chop up the whole plant and use it in cooking for its nourishing components of chlorophyll and vitamin C.

How to Preserve

Dry the plant immediately in a dehydrator or low-temperature oven to prevent it from going to seed. This will allow the plant to harbor its delicate aromatics for use as a nutrient-rich tea. Store in a sealed container after the drying process.

Dry and roast the seeds in a cast-iron skillet to create a coffee-like tea. Store the dried and roasted seeds in a sealed container; grind them just before use and brew in a French press. *Galium* is in the same family as coffee, and the seeds hold a small amount of caffeine.

forest floors beneath the tall cow parsnips and sweet root. Or locate it in lower-elevation shady places, near chickweed or miner's lettuce. The higher you are in elevation, the later you will be able to gather fresh leaves. Lower-elevation plants will go to seed first. Collect seeds in late summer or fall.

How to Gather

Almost all parts of cleavers will stick to you. The plant and the seeds have fine hooked hairs that grab hold of fabric. Cleavers also pulls easily from the ground, which makes you take more than you really need. With a pair of scissors, or pincer fingers, take only the top young whorls from the plant. If you happen to uproot the entire plant, it's okay: utilize it all.

Future Harvests

Cleavers are usually found growing in thick stretches, making it easy to harvest an ample amount of tops without causing a shortage of growth. The clinging burrs are spread easily by passing animals or hikers.

cota

Thelesperma species
greenthread, Navajo tea, Hopi tea

EDIBLE leaves, stems, flowers

Cota is highly regarded as a tea by Native Americans for its lovely taste and medicinal value. It is sold commercially but, as it is one of my favorite wild teas, I would rather find it for free.

How to Identify

Slender green stems arise from a small beige taproot. The entire plant has a glaucous coating, which makes it look somewhat blue-green. Thin, thread-like leaves grow from the base and sporadically along the stem. There may be a dozen stems or a single stem growing from the

Cota's long stalks make it easy to gather and form into bundles.

root, but only one flower sits atop each stalk. Flowers are yellow; some species (e.g., *Thelesperma filifolium*) have both ray and disc flowers, while others (e.g., *T. megapotamicum*) have only disc flowers.

Where and When to Gather

Cota is found in Colorado (primarily in the Navajo Nation and Four Corners area), in Wyoming, and in parts of Montana. Plants inhabit dry soils or open meadows at elevations between 3,500 and 8,000 feet. Flower stems, complete with leaves, are best gathered as the flower buds are beginning to blossom, and when the plant is most fragrant.

How to Gather

The stems and flowers make a beautiful bundle of herb tea. Cut stems about 3 inches above the ground. Then make a simple bundle by folding three to five flowering stems over again and again, until the bundle is about palm size. Fasten the bundle with string, or carefully use another piece of cota stem to wrap it all up.

How to Eat

A refreshing herb tea can be made from the flowers and green portions of cota. It has a mild taste comparable to green tea or chamomile. This tea is divine served iced on a hot summer's day or hot for a soothing day-ender.

How to Preserve

Dried bundles remain flavorful for years but are better if used within one year. A single bundle can make about a quart to two quarts of tea.

Future Harvests

First, make sure not to pull this plant out by its roots. Second, be sure there is adequate foliage left behind when cutting above the ground. This keeps it healthy for the following year.

Caution

Cota is in the Asteraceae, and some people may have allergic reactions to this plant family.

cottonwood

Populus species

poplar

EDIBLE buds, bark, twigs, catkins, cambium

Just when you think winter's grip will never loosen, mighty cotton-woods offer a small treasure. Infuse their buds in honey for a spice and aroma that will pull you through to spring.

Cottonwoods are hardly ever found growing alone and require a lot of water to thrive.

How to Identify

Cottonwood trees have scaly or rough, gray-brown bark with deep furrows and an average height of 50 to 100 feet. Branches may look bare in the winter, but they hold aromatic buds that exude a sweet balsam-scented resin. Leaves are alternate and ovate, lanceolate, or heart-shaped with toothed edges. All *Populus* species are dioecious, meaning the tree is either male or female. The main difference between catkins is the male catkins shed pollen while the female catkins produce the seeds. The cottonwood is cursed by people in the spring for the cotton fluff of its seeds.

Where and When to Gather

Cottonwood trees dominate the riverbanks, irrigated fields, and floodplains of the west. Gather their riches in winter and spring. Collect the sweet-tasting catkins while the tiny flower buds are still closed. Once the whole catkin flowers, it soon becomes just fluff and loses taste, and if you gather them too early, when they are tightly closed, they are likely to be too bitter.

The resinous buds are easy to collect in early spring from wind-fallen branches.

Male catkins dangle from the limbs of cottonwoods, looking something like long caterpillars. They are edible at this stage.

How to Gather

Wind, beavers, and tree trimmers are my three favorite allies when it comes to gathering cottonwood limbs and buds. Find a beaver-fallen tree or a nice spot where many branches have freshly fallen. Sit there and pick through the twigs to collect just the buds. Stay long enough to garble, quietly in nature, if you have the time to surrender yourself. You can also take the branches home for a more thorough collection and for utilizing the twigs, bark, or cambium. The cambium of the bark is essentially a survival food; it's hard to gather enough for calories.

How to Eat

Catkins are a nice nibble on a spring walk, with their complex, sweet and spicy taste. If you find a loaded, low-hanging branch, pick a few handfuls to try out in the kitchen.

How to Preserve

An infused honey of cottonwood buds is a must-try, and it doesn't take too many buds to make such a concoction. Fill any glass jar halfway with the buds. Including small pieces of attached branches is fine. Cover with honey and set in a warm spot to infuse for a week. The spicy-balsam flavor is outrageously good in teas or as a culinary ingredient. Chew on a honeyed bud for a real mouth tantalizer. Bark can be used in teas or extracts for its bitter components.

Future Harvests

Please do not go chopping limbs off of trees for any reason, unless you are pruning your own. Cottonwood branches come down very easily and unexpectedly; there are plenty of fresh downed branches to be found.

cow parsnip

Heracleum maximum

wild celery

EDIBLE leaves, stalks, flower buds, seeds

Young unfurled leaves and budding flowers of cow parsnip are firm and tender when steamed or boiled. They have a flavor reminiscent of parsnip.

How to Identify

Big palmate leaflets, a thick stalk, and showy umbels of white flowers make this carrot-family plant easy to distinguish from all the others. Cow parsnip can grow upward of 9 feet tall, supported by thick, hollow, grooved stems. Both leafstalks and stems are coarse and hairy. The leafstalks too are hollow and grow alternately up the stem. Flowers are carried in an umbel, an umbrella-shaped inflorescence. They are creamy in color with five deeply notched petals; some petals are larger than the others. When the flowers are budding, they form a dense sheathed ball. Flat, widely ovate seeds are highly aromatic. You will rarely find cow parsnip growing alone.

The unfurled leaves are at the perfect stage for harvesting, and they make a pleasing steamed or sautéed vegetable.

The stalks and leafstalks are flavored somewhat like celery. Peel first before eating raw or cooking.

Where and When to Gather

Cow parsnip inhabits damp forests from the foothills to the subalpine regions. A springtime walk in the woods provides the forager with unfurling leaves, flower buds, and tender young stalks. In late spring or early summer the plant sends up a young flowering stalk; the best time to harvest it is before the flower buds blossom.

How to Gather

Wear gloves and cover limbs while harvesting this plant (see caution). Young unfurled leaves can be picked individually by hand. Spread out your harvesting over a generous walk through the timbers, and never strip a plant of all its leaves.

How to Eat

The young leaves and closed flower buds of cow parsnip can be steamed or boiled and

Large palmate leaflets make cow parsnip easy to distinguish from other plants in the Apiaceae.

used as a side vegetable. For stalks to be deemed delicious raw, they should first be peeled. The bare stems taste most similar to celery and can be used as such. Raw stems can be stuffed with nut butters and dried berries, or try cream cheese, minced wild chives, and pickled dandelion buds for an hors d'oeuvre.

How to Preserve

The young unfurled leaves, flower buds, and seeds can be dried and used for their interesting spicy parsnip–like flavors.

Future Harvest

Cow parsnip is readily found throughout the west. Harvest with care, taking a little from each plant.

Caution

Always take extra caution when keying out or identifying a plant with white umbel flowers, because most belong in the Apiaceae, which family contains poison hemlock (*Conium maculatum*) and water hemlock (*Cicuta* species), two of the most toxic plants in North America.

Furocoumarins are found in the sap of the skin and hairs of cow parsnip. An unpleasant dermatitis reaction occurs when the sap is left on skin and can be made worse by exposure to sunlight. For some people this can cause a nasty burn, so it is best to handle the stalks with care or use gloves. Make sure to wash hands or limbs as soon as possible after collecting and processing.

crabapple

Malus species

flowers, fruit

The sweet-and-sour bite of crabapples makes them a nice flavorful addition to jellies or fruit leathers.

How to Identify

There is no greater scent than when all the crabapple trees go into bloom each spring. The scent is sweeter than rose, a floral fragrance that lingers through neighborhood streets. Crabapples look very similar to an apple tree, with rough brown bark and white to fuchsia blossoms. The trees are stout with dense branches bearing leaves that are ovate and lightly serrated or scalloped. Fruits are smaller than 2 inches in diameter, varying in color from yellow-green to pink-red and magenta-orange.

Where and When to Gather

Crabapples are drought-tolerant trees that handle extremely cold temperatures quite well. They can be found in backyards and old town sites, near old buildings and farmhouses. I've noticed some trees take a year off and produce fruit only every other year. More rain during the summer makes

Crabapple flowers come in a variety of colors from white to magenta. You will find most in neighborhoods or town squares; it's very rare to find a feral crabapple tree.

for juicier apples; drought years usually mean mealy fruit. Apples are ready for picking in September and into October. Frost sweetens them, making them soft and more suitable for harvesting.

How to Gather

Get a bushel or basket and start picking. My favorites to gather are the deep red ones that are larger in size or the miniature Braeburn-looking crabapples; these two are slightly sweet, juicy, and sour, making them perfect for cooking or ciders.

How to Eat

Most people find crabapples a little tart straight off the tree, but it definitely depends on the tree as much as the person. Smaller crabapples tend to be the most bitter; larger fruits approach domesticated apples for taste. Crabapples pair nicely with wild plums, wild grapes, and other ripe fruits of the season. Crabapple buds and blossoms make a heavenly tea; try them fresh or dried.

It takes only a few minutes to pick enough crabapples for a large batch of fruit leathers.

Fruit leathers

Fruit leathers are an easy way to preserve your fruit forage in the form of a convenient, sweet, chewy snack.

To begin, fill a pot about halfway with your freshly cleaned fruit and just cover with water. Bring to a boil and turn down to a simmer, while you mash the fruits into smithereens. Cook until this mixture is pureed and thick. If you are using crabapples or another fruit that has undesirable seeds and stems, you will need to strain the mixture. Using a mesh strainer or food mill, press out as much of the mush as you can into another bowl and then transfer the mixture from the bowl to a tray lined with parchment paper. Create thin, even layers. If too thick, it may not dry properly; if too thin, it won't peel off in nice sheets. You can leave this out on the counter to dry over the next few days. To speed up the process, put in a dehydrator at a medium-low setting, or use your oven on its lowest setting. Drying times can vary based on what fruit you use and how thickly you spread the mixture. Once dried, score the mixture into strips, peel off the fruit leathers, and store in a sealed container. Storing in the refrigerator may keep them fresh longer, but there really is no need.

How to Preserve

Crapapples are high in pectin, so fruit leathers and jellies are a cinch to make. Cook crabapples with a little water until they break up and turn to mush; take the hot apple pulp and strain out the seeds for fruit leathers, jellies, butters, and sauces. A food mill also works well to remove the tiny seeds, which are very tedious to remove by hand.

Crabapples also make one heck of a good cider. A friend and I joked that with all the crabapples I gather every year, we could open a cidery. Try pressing the crabapples and fermenting the juice so that you can make hard cider or raw apple cider vinegar. The flowers can be dried for brewing tea. Save dried flowers and, once the fruits are ripe, make a delicious elixir or cordial from both parts of the plant. This can be used as a bitter digestif, before or after meals.

Future Harvests

Most trees have more fruit than their branches can hold or the birds can eat.

dandelion

Taraxacum species

EDIBLE leaves, flower buds, flowers, roots

The dandelion is well recognized around the world. Learn to love its bitter leaves: they are better for you than you know!

How to Identify

Bright yellow flowerheads crop up all over in the springtime, and most of them belong to the beloved dandelion. It looks as though only a single flowerhead, held by a green bract, sits atop the scape, but in fact the bloom consists of hundreds of tiny ray flowers. When broken, the wide and hollow stem (or scape) flows white latex. The leaves are always basal and lobed, having uneven edges like that of a key (or the teeth of a lion—hence the common name, a corruption of the French, *dent de lion*). All leaves form a thick rosette around a taproot that is usually a pale cream color. Several flower stems will arise out of a single rosette. Pappus is the white fluff we see once dandelions have gone to seed.

Where and When to Gather

Finding a clean place to gather dandelions is important; most gardeners will gladly

Before the dandelion blossoms, pick the closed buds and use them for tart bites in salad or pickle them for later.

Dandelion's vibrant yellow blossoms can be seen filling the mountain valleys in early cummer

have you come weed their beds. Just make sure they are not using chemicals or hosting dogs. In the mountains, however, dandelions abound! There is always an abundance of dandelions to be found in pristine conditions where foot traffic is minimal. The first offering the dandelion puts forth each spring are the leaves; next, the tender flower buds and flowers. The root is best in the spring or fall, after the leaves are dying back.

How to Gather

Gather a few leaves from each plant or dig up the whole plant to use the root as well. Flower buds can be pinched off in the center of the rosette. Once the flowers bloom, either take just the head or pluck down at the base of the stem to get the entire scape as well.

How to Eat

Leaves can be munched on fresh, as a salad; if they are too bitter, mix in some more mild field greens. Cooking the leaves takes out some of the bitterness; dandelion leaves accompany stinging nettles or mustard greens nicely in a sauté of butter with garlic. Flowerheads are excellent dipped and fried in tempura batter or chickpea batter for dandelion pakoras. I find the roots can be a little too bitter to cook with; however, they make a fabulous tea.

How to Preserve

Leaves can be blanched and frozen for future use. The leaves can also be dried and stored for tea or an addition to smoothies. Roots can be dried or pickled. Roasted roots make a nice full-bodied tea. Dry finely chopped roots and then roast them before storing in a glass jar. I like to grind my dried roasted roots just before steeping them in a French press for at least 15 minutes. Add a dollop of acorn-infused butter for a real tasty treat. The flower buds can be pickled to replicate capers and used in classic Italian recipes like puttanesca sauce or chicken marsala.

Future Harvests

Forever and always, dandelions will be considered weeds. They come and go, and we should take better advantage of harvesting them with the seasons. No worries on overharvesting these abundant plants.

Caution

Dandelions are in the Asteraceae, and some people may have allergic reactions to this plant family.

dock

Rumex species

curly dock, yellow dock, cañaigre

EDIBLE leaves, seeds, roots

The tart leaves and crunchy protein-packed seeds of dock can both be cherished ingredients in a summer's salad.

How to Identify

Docks can be spotted from afar by the tall, unbranched, dark brown stalks and seedheads of the previous year. Plants can grow quite large, reaching about 3 feet tall. Leaves are long, thick, and lanceolate; they form a basal rosette in spring. The stalk is jointed, and smaller leaves grow

Dock at this stage of maturity has leaves that are very bitter and astringent.

Seedheads of dock start to dry out in midsummer.

alternately along it. The small flowers are green, red, or brown, and turn into winged seeds. Roots can be quite large and are cream or yellow in color.

Crispy dock (*Rumex crispus*) has curly or wavy edges and is one of the more palatable of the dock species. Western dock (*R. occidentalis*) is abundant throughout the west and has large leaves that have a minimal astringency. The leaves of wild rhubarb (*R. hymenosepalus*) are toxic and should not be eaten.

Where and When to Gather

Find dock growing in sunny fields, canyons, vacant lots, on hillsides, close to ditches, or at the edges of forests. Gather the young leaves in the spring; they toughen up and turn more tart come summer. Seeds and roots can be gathered in the fall.

How to Gather

Gather the young spring leaves by snapping or trimming the leaves from the base. The younger growing leaves along the stalk can be harvested as well. Gather seeds on a dry day. Strip the seedheads from the stalk into a paper bag. Dry seeds by spreading them on a flat surface for a few days or use a dehydrator. Dig roots after the plant has gone to seed; clean well and chop into small pieces for drying.

How to Eat

Dock leaves are full of sour, tart, and astringent flavors that marry well minced on pizzas, torn into salads, or blended with other cooked greens. Dock greens can be boiled in one or two changes of water if the bitterness or astringency is too much. Use these cooked greens in lasagna or blend into quiches or frittatas. Greens are high in vitamin A, calcium, potassium, and iron.

Seeds can be roasted or ground into flour for creating crackers and granolas or added whole to dishes for a protein-rich crunch. Use a 1:1 ratio of ground dock seeds to your flour of choice and a hefty pinch of salt. Add enough water to create a thick pliable, non-sticky paste. Roll out dough and cut to shape before laying the precooked crackers on a greased baking sheet. Bake at 375 degrees Fahrenheit for 10 to 15 minutes to create a wild gourmet cracker. Try adding amaranth and other wild seeds and the pollen of pine or cattail.

Roots are high in iron and can be boiled along with dandelion roots to create a strong decoction. After this brew is strained, add molasses for even more iron fortification.

How to Preserve

Dock leaves can be blanched and frozen. Once the seeds are totally dry, they can be stored in a sealed container. The roots will store in the refrigerator for a few weeks while fresh; chop finely and dry thoroughly before storing in an airtight container.

Future Harvests

Gathering the seeds or leaves from the docks is fine. Most docks are invasive.

Caution

Docks are high in oxalic acid, which, if consumed in large quantities, can cause gastric upset or greatly affect people who suffer from kidney disease and stones.

Douglas fir

Pseudotsuga menziesii

EDIBLE young tips, needles, resin

The young tips of Douglas fir have a fresh lemony flavor that's perfect for smoking fish or blending into teas.

How to Identify

Douglas firs are great evergreen conifers averaging 100 feet when mature. The bark is gray, becoming thicker and darker with age. Smooth bark of young trees will eventually turn rough and crack as the tree gets older. Soft, flat, blue-green needles grow in an alternating spiral along the branch. Douglas firs are different from "true" fir trees in that their cones hang from branches; these cones can also be found on the ground. *Abies* species, which are the true firs, have cones that sit erect on branches and disintegrate while there. Cones of a Douglas fir are 2 to 3 inches long and light brown. Distinctive upward-bent, three-pronged bracts are situated between the scales of the cone.

Doug firs have flat needles and unique cones that have little winged bracts between their scales.

Where and When to Gather

Find Douglas fir on mountain slopes from Colorado north, and west all the way to the Pacific Coast of northern California, Oregon, and Washington. The needles of any conifer can be gathered year-round, though I find the young, spring tips of Douglas fir and spruces to be the best. The resins are best gathered when they are flowing up or down the tree in spring and fall, while soft and gooey.

How to Gather

Find a forest full of Douglas fir and meander among trees, plucking only a few tips from each. The tips are the new growth at the ends of branches. Needles can be stripped from fallen branches.

How to Eat

Use needles in tea blends or to enhance the flavor of smoked sea salt (see sidebar on page 179). Place small branch trimmings on top of wild-caught trout before baking or smoking; this will cook in an essence of Douglas fir. Create an infused butter with the minced young tips and use this for baking cookies or slathering on toast.

A simple syrup can be made of the spring tips by simmering them in water and sugar. After straining them out, add a handful or two of fresh tips to the syrup. Heat to a simmer again for a few minutes, and then strain them out. Dust the tips with sugar and place them on a baking sheet covered in parchment paper. Turn your oven to the lowest heat setting and place the tray of candied tips inside for a few hours, until crispy. This candied treat is a beautiful garnish to desserts.

How to Preserve

An infused olive oil of fir tips is divine. It can be drizzled over just about anything.

Future Harvests

Harvesting fir tips, when spread out through many trees, will not impede the growth of a particular tree.

elderberry

Sambucus species

EDIBLE flowers, fruit

There is nothing more intoxicating than the smell of a room full of elderflowers drying in the spring.

How to Identify

The leaves of elder are pinnate with an odd number of leaflets, commonly three to nine, resulting in a leaflet at the tip of the leaf. Leaflets are paired opposite one another along a pithy stem. They are serrated and are mostly lanceolate in shape but can be ovate. The leaves have a musky, unpleasant odor when rubbed; the leaves of the only look-alike, mountain ash, do not. Flowers are white with five petals and five stamens. The inflorescence can be branched with flat-topped clusters, or flowers can form a pyramidal shape. Black or blue elderberry species bear the berries worth harvesting. They are found throughout this mountainous region, just not as densely or commonly as red elderberry (*Sambucus racemosa*).

The white flower clusters of elderberry are not only highly aromatic but also make a delicious fritter.

Black or blue elderberries are the ones worth harvesting.

Where and When to Gather

Find elders growing throughout the Front Range of the Rockies, north to Alberta and Saskatchewan, and westward, in mixed forests, along hillsides, and in meadows. They prefer partial shade and damp soils. Many ornamental elder trees grace neighborhoods, parks, or other landscaped areas that are free from being sprayed. Gather the flowers in late spring or early summer.

How to Gather

Flowers of all *Sambucus* species can be used interchangeably. Clip the flower stem under the first branch of the inflorescence. The fresh stems of elderberry are toxic, and all parts should be removed before processing the flowers or berries. Dry the flowers while they are on the stem. Once dried, garble through the stems, removing the individual flowers. The fruits of red, black, and blue elderberries contain seeds that are also toxic if they are not cooked or dried, so don't be tempted in the field (or spit them out if you want to taste).

How to Eat

The flowers can be turned into champagne, cordials, and simple syrup; infused into vodka; or battered and cooked into fritters. Make a hydrosol or infused honey from the fresh flowers picked off the stems.

Red elderberries can be eaten cooked. The raw red berries are said to make people nauseous and cause stomach discomfort.

Caution with the red berries—sample them only after being cooked. I am not a fan of the flavor, so I only use the flowers of red elder. People do use cooked red elders in jellies and sauces.

If using fresh berries, whatever their color, run them through a food mill first to remove all the seeds. Use fresh berries in fruit salads or to top desserts. Bake berries into pies, crepes, and muffins. The berries can be infused into alcohols, for cocktail concoctions or blending into cordials, and elixirs. Mash and cook berries into juice for wines, simple syrups, jellies, and sorbet. Infuse berries into honey or vinegar for use in a multitude of cooking endeavors.

How to Preserve

Flowers and berries can be dried or dehydrated and used in teas, which are perfect wintertime tonics.

Future Harvests

Before you get overly excited about gathering elderflowers from the new stand you found, remember that removing all the flowers and buds means no berries will be produced.

Caution

Leaves, seeds, and stems are toxic and should not be ingested while fresh. Red elderberries should only be eaten after being cooked.

filaree

Erodium cicutarium

stork's bill, alfilaria, redstem filaree

EDIBLE leaves, roots

Use the tart leaves of filaree in salsas and pesto, or as a minced garnish atop soups and salads.

How to Identify

Leaves are a rich green, reaching at most 6 inches long; they are pinnate and highly dissected, with a soft sticky fuzz. The first leaves spread out in a flattened basal rosette. Leaves will grow taller in more fertile, longer-seasoned growing conditions. In the mountain west, the plant usually remains under a foot tall. Stems are hairy, and flowers are bright pink with five petals. Seeds can be a nuisance, especially when they burrow into the thick fur of my Alaskan malamute. They have a sharp seedhead with a long corkscrewed tail. This is for the seed's survival: once a seed has landed on the ground, the wind gently turns its corkscrewed tail, forcing the seed into the earth.

Where and When to Gather

Find filaree well established in the mountain west as a nonnative plant. It does

Another common name for filaree is stork's bill, a reference to the long pointed seedpod, which resembles the beak of a stork or heron. *Erodios* actually means "heron" in Greek, hence *Erodium*.

Rosettes of filaree bunched close together.

extremely well in harsh climates with intense sun, arid land, and even extreme cold. Filaree also thrives in partial sun, grasslands, and moist climates. Gather the leaves in spring or the roots all year long.

How to Gather

Pick young leaves or pull up the whole plant to have access to the sweet root.

How to Eat

The young leaves are best, having a somewhat sweet and tart taste. They do well in salads, in spring pesto spreads, or garnishing sandwiches and wraps. The root can be chewed on to release its sweet flavors. It has been called Hopi candy as the children of that tribe used it like gum. Older leaves, though more bitter, can still be used and are suitable for soups, sauces, or stews.

Future Harvests

Filaree is considered a noxious weed, and its seeds spread very easily, usually by sticking to your clothes or dog companions. Feel free to dig up the whole plant and experiment with the sweet-tasting root. Just be sure you are harvesting in an area that is not being sprayed for the removal of this plant.

Caution

The species epithet is a reference to *Cicuta* (water hemlock), for the similarity of their leaves, and the two plants can grow close together. I find the leaves to be very different, however, and the stem of filaree is hairy (in *Cicuta* species, it is not).

fir

Abies species

EDIBLE young tips, needles, resin

Firs have complex fragrances and flavors—deliciously subtle hints of balsam or lemon—that are readily captured in teas or honey.

How to Identify

Firs are best identified by their cones, which grow in the upper branches, so you will have to look high up in the tree to notice them. They sit on top of the branches, like so many baby owls, and point toward the sky. Cones disintegrate while on the tree; if you happen to find one

Notice the flat needles on this white fir (*Abies concolor*).

Infused oils

Pick oil that works for you in your kitchen. I like to use coconut and olive oils best. If using fresh herb, chop the plant and let it wilt for a day before using it. This releases moisture trapped in the plant. Skip this step if your plant matter is dry. Next, fill a jar about halfway with the chopped herb. Fill the remainder of the jar with oil, leaving 2 inches to the rim. Leave the jar uncovered so any trapped water from the plant can evaporate out of the oil. Set the uncovered jar in a sunny windowsill, or create a double boiler. Make a double boiler by filling a pan with water, creating a water bath for your jar of herb oil. If using the windowsill method, let your plant matter steep in the oil for a week or two. When using the double boiler, use the lowest stovetop or crockpot setting; your herbs should infuse for eight to 48 hours. Whatever method you choose, stir the oil infusion, when you remember, to release air bubbles. Strain your herbs well when infusion is complete.

If you used fresh herb, another step will need to happen before storage. Allow your jar of strained oil to sit on the counter for three to seven days, until you see a filmy layer in the bottom of the jar. This is the water trapped in the oil. You do not want this in your final product, so you must decant. Do this by pouring the top oil out into a clean glass jar, and leaving the filmy white sludge behind. For a prolonged shelf life, store this oil in the refrigerator, taking spoonfuls out as needed. To increase the life span, store your jar in the freezer.

on the ground, it is probably from an animal knocking it down. All firs have flat needles, and you can notice this when you try to roll the needle between your fingers. Mountain alpine fir (*Abies bifolia*) has a single white line on the dorsal side of the needle and two beneath, while white fir (*A. concolor*) has two white lines only on the underside of the needle. The cones differ in color as well: mountain alpine fir cones are a dark purple-gray, while white fir cones vary from a golden green to purple.

Where and When to Gather
Find firs growing in subalpine mountain forests or up at treeline. Gather the young tips of the branches in late spring or the needles all year long.

How to Gather
Pick the bright green soft tips off various branches, tasting each tree to find the flavors you like best. White fir has a lemony scent and flavor, while mountain alpine fir has more of a strong balsam aroma.

How to Eat

Fir tips can be used to infuse a host of culinary ingredients. Start with a fir-tip-and-resin-infused oil or vinegar. For a pleasing simple syrup, simmer the tips in water and sugar. Fir tips can also be candied. After straining out the tips from your warm simple syrup, reheat the syrup and simmer another few handfuls of fresh fir tips for a few minutes. Strain the fir tips and dust in sugar; let them sit out on parchment paper to dry, or speed up the process by placing them in the oven, on the lowest setting. A few hours should crisp them up. Do be careful not to let them burn!

How to Preserve

Candied fir tips can be stored in the freezer for future use in decorating cakes and pies. Get creative and blend the young tips with sea salt to make an infused salt that can be sprinkled atop eggs or fillets of fish or steak.

Future Harvests

Taking needles and tips should not damage the tree. Spread out your harvest of young tips between many trees, simply pruning the forest.

fireweed

Chamerion species
willowherb

EDIBLE shoots, leaves, stalks, flower buds, flowers

After a devastating wildfire, fireweed springs up to cover the ashes. It reestablishes the flora and helps increase food supply for bees, humans, and other animals, offering nutrient-rich shoots and leaves and delightfully aromatic flowers.

How to Identify

Fireweed is a staple wildflower of the west, growing erect with four-petaled fuchsia flowers blossoming from the bottom up to the tip of the raceme. They say that once the last of the flowers blossom, the first snow is days aways. Young shoots of fireweed can be noticed in the spring, poking through old leaves, next to the first yarrow and dandelion leaves. The young stalks have a reddish coloring that disperses into the green leaves. Stem and leaves are both smooth and hairless. The leaves are long and lanceolate; some have slightly toothed margins and look similar to willow leaves. Each leaf has a pronounced white midvein and spirals alternately up the thick stem.

Where and When to Gather

Obviously, old burn sites are a common place to find fireweed thriving. It likes the cool, moist mountain air and is usually found at the edges of woods, in pasturelands, near waterways, high on rocky slopes, or along roadsides. Start gathering in late spring.

How to Gather

Spring shoots of fireweed may best be identified if previously marked with a rock while the plant is in bloom the previous year. Snap or snip off the reddish shoots at least an inch from the ground. Before all the flowers bloom, clip off the top portion of the budding raceme.

How to Eat

Shoots of fireweed can be eaten raw or cooked lightly by steaming or sautéing. They are somewhat crunchy and just a touch mucilaginous. Young leaves can be eaten raw. The older vibrant leaves can be used as a cooked green or dried for tea consumption. Flower bud racemes can be boiled or steamed for a slightly sweet side vegetable. The delicate sweet citrusy aroma of the flowers is a nice touch strewn upon salads. Any segment of the stalk can be peeled or sliced long ways in half for easy access to the sweet pith. The flowers are great suppliers of nectar for our honeybees so if you ever stumble upon fireweed honey, then you are in luck. Its pungency is impeccable.

Fireweed is a testimonial of endurance and the dwindling days of summer. Quick, before the first snowflakes fall—clip the top 3 inches of the unbloomed flower raceme and eat raw or cooked.

The young shoots of fireweed at the perfect stage for harvesting in late spring or early summer.

How to Preserve

Young shoots can be blanched and keep well frozen for up to six months. Flowers can be used to make florally sweet jelly or candies; the color they produce is absolutely stunning. When making the jelly, be sure to add a touch of lemon juice; the acidity really brings out the color, as does the addition of pectin.

Future Harvests

Clipping the shoots back in early spring helps to stimulate growth, so no need to worry about overharvesting the shoots. Be mindful of the other early growth around you in the spring by walking with care.

glacier lily
Erythronium grandiflorum
avalanche lily

EDIBLE leaves, flowers, bulbs

Soon after the snow melts in spring, yellow glacier lilies flood mountain meadows with their sweet honey-tasting flowers.

How to Identify

Glacier lilies are one of the first flowers to spring up after the long winter's snow cover finally melts, their yellow six-tepaled blossoms nodding to the ground below. The stem can vary in length, supporting one or two bent-over flowers. A single pair of narrowly oblong or elliptic leaves arises from the bulb (technically, a corm). Leaves are glossy, smooth, and vibrantly green. The higher the plant grows in elevation, the more dwarf it becomes.

Where and When to Gather

Walk through a high mountain meadow in late spring, and with any luck, glacier lilies will delight you. Find them growing in the partial shade of forests, in sunny high alpine meadows, and in avalanche slide paths.

The yellow flowers of glacier lilies, so worth seeing and foraging, will be missed if you do not travel to the alpine in spring.

Hillsides and mountain meadows can be loaded with these cheery spring flowers.

How to Gather

Pluck off budding and bloomed flowers. Glacier lilies are usually found growing closely together in large stands, making it easy to dig up a few corms at a time. The corms can be fairly deep in the earth, so dig gently, using a digging stick or tool to loosen the soil.

How to Eat

Glacier lilies are among the most beautiful edible spring flowers. Use them to garnish fruit cocktails or any other dish, for that matter: their curved petals help latch the flower onto the sides of any glass or bowl, and the fragrant honey-scented flowers make the best floating accompaniment to awe-inspiring martinis. The leaves can be eaten as well but are not my favorite in texture; they are best used sparingly, minced up and spread throughout a salad. Corms of the glacier lily can be eaten raw or cooked; they have a somewhat sweet and pleasantly crisp bite.

How to Preserve

The corms can be dried and reconstituted in soups.

Future Harvests

Glacier lilies take upward of seven years to reach full maturity; digging up roots in quantity may be unsustainable in areas of the Rocky Mountains. Only if the plant vastly surrounds you is it okay to dig a few corms to taste, or enough for a small meal. Take only small harvests of the entire plant, and again, only where it is growing very abundantly.

golden currant
Ribes aureum

EDIBLE fruit

The sweet and sour flavors of golden currants are a pleasure worth seeking on a hot, late summer's day.

How to Identify

Yellow tubular flowers give golden currant its name, not the immature yellow berries. Golden currant berries are shiny, smooth, and can be black, golden orange, or red when ripe. Like most *Ribes* berries, the dried flower will be left on the base of the berry, giving each berry a little tail. This woody shrub grows to 6 feet and generally has entirely spineless branches. The leaves have deep clefts (they look like small maple leaves) and turn deep red in autumn. Clove currant (*R. aureum* var. *villosum*) has more aromatic flowers; they smell like clove and vanilla in the spring.

Where and When to Gather

Gather the berries in late summer or early fall. Find them used abundantly in landscaping, or growing wild in damp soils, forest floors, riparian areas, and canyon bottoms throughout the mountain west.

The tubular flowers of golden currant are yellow.

Golden currant berries can be black, golden orange, or red when ripe.

How to Gather

Clip the hanging fruit cluster to make gathering easy. You can either process the berries while they are fresh, or freeze them first to make popping them off the stem a breeze. Don't bother taking off the flower remnants; it is tedious work that goes unnoticed.

How to Eat

Enjoy golden currants fresh or dried over muesli with strawberries, raspberries, amaranth seeds, and other wild ingredients. Berries can be mashed and simmered in a little water to be spread out and dried as fruit leathers. Add more water to your mash and strain, and then add some sweetener to make juice or syrup. Ice cream, sorbet, pie filling, and wine can all be made from these delicious little berries.

How to Preserve

Freeze, dehydrate, or preserve golden currant's scrumptious flavor in a jelly or jam. Use dried golden currants in place of raisins in rice pilaf or among cooked wild greens and pine nuts.

Future Harvests

Other than snatching berries from birds, I do not see any issues with harvesting golden currants.

goldenrod

Solidago species

leaves, flower buds, flowers

Seek out the unbloomed flowerheads of goldenrod for a tender, wild, broccolini-like vegetable.

How to Identify

When in full bloom, goldenrod's flowers light up the fence lines with their crescent-shaped heads of clustered yellow flowers. Plants range in height (some grow just shy of a foot, while others grow over 7 feet tall), and they form large stands: where there is one, there are usually many. The stalk is unbranched, and in some species it can be hairy, along with the leaves. Long, lanceolate leaves grow up the stalk alternately. Some leaves have smooth edges, while others are jagged. Many people blame hay fever on goldenrod, but it

The tightly closed flowerheads of goldenrod are perfect for pinching off under the inflorescence and steaming or boiling like little broccolinis.

Goldenrod's yellow flowers are a beacon, carried high, from mid- to late summer. The color reminds us all that fall is coming and that the matching color of school buses will be cruising the streets again soon.

is a completely innocent bystander, as it is not wind-pollinated.

Where and When to Gather

Goldenrod inhabits disturbed soils, in partial to full sun, and can be located in fields, along riverbanks, and high up mountain roads. Several species occur throughout the mountain west; all are usually fully bloomed by August in most elevations, so prime harvesting season begins in July or early summer.

How to Gather

Goldenrod is entirely edible: gather the leaves, florets, and flowers. Young florets can be harvested by pinching off the top few inches of the plant before the flowers bloom, while the buds are still closed. Harvest leaves by taking a few from each plant, not stripping the stalk.

How to Eat

Enjoy as a broccolini substitute; the tender unbloomed flowerheads can be steamed, sautéed, or boiled. Leaves can be added to any dish raw or cooked. The leaves and flowers make a slightly bitter, astringent, and aromatic tea.

How to Preserve

Flowers and leaves can be infused into honey. The leaves dry up well for future soothing teas, but the flowers do not, as they poof out and go to seed.

Future Harvests

This plant spreads by its roots, so there are no implications with harvesting the flowering tops. The plant will stay happy as long as it has most of its leaves left intact.

gooseberry
Ribes species

EDIBLE fruit

High summer is usually the start of gooseberry season, and my favorite way to enjoy their tart juiciness is straight from their thorny thickets.

How to Identify

Plants are shrubs, with tall arching branches thickly set. Leaves are intricately lobed, varying slightly from plant to plant, sometimes looking like a small maple leaf. Flowers are trumpet-shaped, blossoming downward toward the ground. As with all *Ribes* species, gooseberries hold onto the remnants of each flower's sepals at the tip of the berry. Both currants and gooseberries can have thorny stems; one way to tell them apart is that gooseberry stems come off attached to the berry and currants don't. Gooseberry fruit also tends to have a bit more of a sour-grape flavor than currants.

The skin of plump gooseberries can appear translucent. When immature, the berries are green, yellow, or red, with light vertical lines, making them look like a

Green gooseberries are full of pectin and can be picked before turning ripe to use for setting jellies and jams.

Gooseberries are easy to pick, so long as your hands are agile and dodge the thorns.

striped marble. All the gooseberries in this region—white-stem gooseberry (*Ribes inerme*), trumpet gooseberry (*R. leptanthum*), and Canadian gooseberry (*R. oxyacanthoides*)—turn dark blue or blackish purple at maturity.

Where and When to Gather

Gooseberries begin to ripen in July, and you can find fruit through early fall if you go up into the mountains. Look for the shrubby thickets at the border of a forest or tucked near waterways.

How to Gather

Individually pluck each berry and put it directly in your mouth or come up with a more strategic plan, such as laying a tarp under the bush and shaking the branches or hitting them with a stick. Do be mindful of the thorns; they can snag both your clothes and your skin.

How to Eat

Fresh off the bush is best. If you can bring some home, toss them into salads for a crisp tart bite or into curried rice dishes for an added sweetness.

Gooseberries make a delicious grapey juice. Cook the berries with some water on a low temperature while mashing them up. Strain out the pulp, and enjoy the juice, sweetened with sugar or honey. This is also the first step to creating simple syrup or jelly that can be simmered down after the sweetener is added. Let the simple syrup be the base for sorbets and specialty drinks. Green gooseberries, though much more tart than ripe berries, are loaded with pectin and can be used to make jams or fruit fillings without the use of commercial pectin.

How to Preserve

Berries can be canned into jams and jellies, or the berries can be frozen for later consumption. Gooseberry simple syrup is a lovely condiment to add to margaritas or martinis. Fruit leathers are another great way to preserve this puckery berry, although you may want to add honey or sugar to the pulp before drying. Whole berries can be dried or dehydrated and stored for a raisin-like treat.

Future Harvests

Picking berries will not affect future harvests, but wildlife may depend on them for food, so always leave some berries behind. Gooseberries transplant well from cuttings, if you want to try growing some in your own garden.

A handful of ripe gooseberries on a midsummer's day.

ground cherry

Physalis species

tomatillo, husk tomato

EDIBLE fruit

Keep your eyes peeled for the lantern-like husks of ground cherries, tucked under fall foliage. You may be surprised by the sweet juiciness of this little fruit.

How to Identify

The bright green foliage of ground cherry can be found sprawling on the ground or standing almost 3 feet erect. Some *Physalis* species have fine hairs on the alternate leaves. Flowers are yellow bells, nodding toward the earth. The inner center of the flower can have purple splotches. Fruits develop in a bladder-like husk that looks like a lantern. The cherry-shaped fruits are green when immature and turn a golden yellow when ripe.

Where and When to Gather

Ground cherries are found throughout the mountain west, usually at lower elevations but occasionally as high as 8,000 feet. They do extremely well in sunny, poor, sandy soils or fields, but don't be surprised to find them in forests and on hillsides with partial shade. Begin gathering the fruits in the fall.

How to Gather

If you happen to pick some unripe fruits in late summer, it's okay. If you leave them in the husk, they will ripen off the plant. Ground cherries are notorious for falling to the ground before ripe. Pick these up first. If they are still green-yellow, wait a few days to a week for them to ripen into a deep golden orange-yellow before consuming. Make sure the berries are a little tart and sweet, not bitter. Do not eat green, unripe ground cherries.

How to Eat

Ground cherries can be eaten raw or cooked. Try them in salads of any sort, or add to roasted root dishes to perk them up. Fruits have a sweetness that lends itself well to pies, fruit leathers, syrups, and tarts. Ground cherries can be made into sweet and spicy salsas when prepared with fresh mango, cilantro, and habanero peppers.

How to Preserve

If fruits are left in the husk, ground cherries can be stored over winter in the refrigerator. Sliced fruits can be dehydrated and stored for later use in baked goods. Blend ground cherries together with crabapples, wild plums, and other fall fruits to make marmalades, chutneys, and jams.

Harvest the dried papery husks of ground cherry in the fall, and find the pleasant ripe orange-yellow fruit that waits inside.

Future Harvests

This perennial plant reproduces easily from the seeds of fallen fruit and is usually found in abundance. Your foraging will not affect its continuance.

Caution

Eat the inner golden yellow fruit only when it is ripe and not bitter. The husk of the fruit is toxic, as is the immature green fruit. As the plant is a member of the nightshade family, all the foliage of ground cherries is toxic as well.

hackberry

Celtis species

sugarberry

EDIBLE fruit

Hackberries have a taste and texture that mirror this arid-loving tree's habitat—a little bit of dry, sweet flesh and a bunch of crunch.

How to Identify

Hackberry trees are known for their knobby, corky, layered bark. Trees are on the small side, reaching a peak height of 30 feet. The leaves are ovate to lanceolate, with one side longer than the other, and an uneven base, making them look slightly crescent-shaped. Leaves are alternately arranged and are serrate or entire around the margins. The fruit of a hackberry isn't considered a berry but rather a drupe. They hang singly from a stem and have a hard-shelled nut that is rather large for the size of berry, yielding a small amount of flesh. The ripe berries of netleaf hackberry (*Celtis reticulata*) turn from green to red; common hackberry (*C. occidentalis*) ends with a darker-colored berry.

Small berries can be hard to see unless you take a closer look at the tree. They are ripe once they have turned red.

The bark of a hackberry tree has a distinctive warty texture.

Where and When to Gather

Hackberry is found in the lower elevations and foothills of the mountain west, preferring the long summers and a dry climate. It does best when it is close to rivers or streams. Find it planted as a landscape ornamental, at a park, or in someone's yard. Gather the berries after the first frost, which sweetens them somewhat.

How to Gather

Spread a sheet under the tree, stretching it wide enough to catch the small fruits that will fall from the ends of the branches. This is the best way to gather quantity, if you have the patience to let the fruit fall on its own throughout autumn. If you are merely looking for a snack or want them fast, pick them individually by the handful.

How to Eat

Using a mortar and pestle, smash up the ripe berries. They'll turn into a dough-like substance that is thick, sweet, and crunchy, from the nutshells. If you don't mind the crunch, the hackberry dough is completely edible this way. Mix this into cookies or roll into cinnamon rolls for a sweet inner layer. Another way to enjoy the dry-sweetness of hackberries is to make a "milk" out of it. Use about a 1:2 or 1:3 ratio of hackberries to boiling water, and pour into a blender. Blend until pureed, and add a pinch of sea salt and linden-flower-infused honey or other flavoring. Blend once more before straining through a muslin cloth bag. Enjoy hot or cold.

How to Preserve

Hackberries hold very little moisture. To dry, lay them flat on a tray for a few weeks. They may be frozen fresh for future use.

Future Harvests

Harvesting the hackberries will do no harm to the tree, and plenty will be left high in the trees for squirrels.

hawthorn

Crataegus species

haw, maythorne

EDIBLE fruit

Hawthorn berries vary greatly in size, color, and taste throughout the mountain west. Most hold large amounts of pectin, making them a perfect addition to thicken jellies or jams made from assorted wild fruits.

How to Identify

Approximately six species of *Crataegus* inhabit the mountain west. A deciduous tree or shrub, hawthorn produces either red or black berries with large, hard seeds. Some berries are large enough that they resemble crabapples, but you'll know they're not by the large 1- to 2-inch thorns that embellish most branches of hawthorn. Leaves are ovate, with either subtle jagged edges or lobes or definably larger serrations around the tip. Small white flowers bloom in clusters; each has five petals, resembling a miniature apple blossom.

You will know *Crataegus rivularis*, an abundant hawthorn of the mountain west, by its red ripe berries and unlobed leaves.

Hawthorns grow in thickets; fortunately for foragers, it is rare to see just one shrub growing alone.

Where and When to Gather

Hawthorns are found near riverbanks, on the forested hills of the mountains, and in thickets through canyons. Rarely is a single tree found growing alone, which makes it easy to collect an abundance of berries. The red or black berries begin to ripen in late August or September, depending on your location and elevation.

How to Gather

Pick clusters of berries from the trees being sure to mind the long thorns that adorn most branches. If you find most berries are too high to reach, spread a blanket or sheet around the base of the tree and shake the ripe berries down.

How to Eat

The easiest way to process hawthorns is to cook the berries down in water, creating a pulpy mass, which can then be screened to remove the hard seeds. Otherwise, remove the seeds while berries are fresh by hand or with a food mill. The berries are full of pectin, which comes in very handy when making fruit leathers, sauces, and jellies. They are also high in flavonoids and antioxidants, making them a nutritious choice for pies and strudels.

How to Preserve

The berries can be dried whole before storing in the tea cupboard or ground into a powder after drying. Combine the berry powder with other baking flours such as wheat, coconut, or almond for its pink hue and sweet flavor; it's a sure way to get nutritional benefits in a variety of baked goods. Fruits can also be brewed along with wild apples and crabapples to produce a well-balanced dry hard cider.

Future Harvests

Harvesting berries has no impact on the survival of hawthorn trees, but remember to leave some for the birds and other animals.

hyssop

Agastache species

leaves, flowers, seeds

Coming upon a sun-warmed stand of hyssop, alive with buzzing insects and the sweet smell of anise, is a real treat. Chew on a leaf for more of nature's bounty, the subtle taste of licorice.

How to Identify

When you encounter hyssop in your wanderings, you may think it is mint or possibly catnip on steroids, with its square stems. Giant hyssops can grow to 3 feet or more. When you smell a crushed leaf, you will notice it isn't mint-like but mustier—like catnip with a hint of licorice. Leaves

Experience the aromatics of hyssop by taking a whiff of the flower or by crushing a leaf.

Find hyssop growing in large stands in mountain meadows that receive full sun.

are wider at the base, ovate, and toothed all the way to the tip. Flowers become whiter as they are exposed to the hot sun, whereas the newly bloomed spikes are light pink or lavender. The flowering spike never seems to bloom entirely at once. Upon closer inspection, you will notice the trumpet shape of the flowers and the extra long stamens and stigmas peeking out. The most common hyssop in the Rocky

Mountains is nettleleaf giant hyssop (*Agastache urticifolia*), which has leaves that look like stinging nettle without the stingers. Foliage and seeds of anise hyssop (*A. foeniculum*) have a more pungent flavor of anise, but this plant is scarce throughout the Rockies; it is more common in gardens.

Where and When to Gather

Hyssop begins to blossom in late spring at lower elevations or early summer higher up in the mountains. Look for it in lush mountain meadows and in the partial shade of woodlands. I like to gather the plant when it is in full bloom, putting forth its aromatic budding flowers. Leaves start to lose their flavor from the heat of summer; they are best gathered early in that season.

How to Gather

Pinch or cut off some of the flowering stalk and some leaves. Take only a little from each plant in a large stand. When the flowers are fading in the summer heat and the plant has mostly turned to seed, gather the tops and shake out the seeds.

How to Eat

I like to chew on the leaves and flowers while hiking, for their anise flavor. Fresh leaves can be chopped up and added to salsa and salads, or as a garnish to soups. Fresh seeds can be simmered into simple syrup for soda and cocktail creations. Use seeds as a substitute flavoring where fennel or anise is required; blend them into meatballs or homemade sausage. Tisanes can be made from fresh or dried leaves and flowers. Hyssop is a great wintertime tea; it can also be infused into honey.

How to Preserve

Bundle hyssop stalks with a rubber band and hang upside down to let the herb dry. After drying, crumble leaves and flowers off the stalks. Store the crushed hyssop in a sealed jar, and its aromatics will be preserved for future tisanes.

Future Harvests

The reason you never see only one hyssop plant is because it spreads through underground rhizomes. Since the plant is not spreading strictly by seed, it's okay to gather flowering heads. Be respectful of the pollinating insects, and leave plenty of flowers behind.

juniper
Juniperus species

leaves, fruit

Juniper berries provide the forager chef with a pungent woodsy flavor that pairs nicely with wild meats, tempering their gamey flavor.

The best time to harvest is when the berries are still somewhat chalky but have turned royal to dark blue. This is the sprawling, shrub-like *Juniperus communis*.

Juniper berries can be harvested throughout the winter months.

How to Identify

Juniper grows in two ways, as a ground-dwelling shrub or as a trunked tree. Branches have scaly evergreen leaves that are rough or needle-like. The berries are really soft, flesh-covered cones. All species of juniper have green immature berries that ripen to a chalky deep royal blue. Common species of the mountain west are Utah juniper (*Juniperus osteosperma*), common juniper (*J. communis*), and Rocky Mountain juniper (*J. scopulorum*).

Where and When to Gather

Junipers can be found all over the mountain west and southwestern Canada. Find them growing in landscaped yards or clinging to canyon walls. Juniper likes a dry climate, growing alongside piñon or sagebrush. The best time to gather is when juniper berries reach a royal blue color in late fall or early spring. Branch tips and leaves can be collected all year.

How to Gather

I gather juniper berries by raking my fingers through the leaves, releasing the berries into a basket I hold below. Clip the branch tips and take some leaves when gathering the berries.

How to Eat

Junipers add welcome, rosemary-y flavor to poultry, elk, antelope, venison, and other wild game meats. Fresh or dried berries can be crushed with pepperweed seeds and sea salt for a rub to coat the meat with prior to cooking. Try also adding different wild ingredients that are native to your surroundings—beebalm, wild onions, the berries of skunkbush, smooth sumac, or mountain ash—to make a region-specific rub, marinade, or brine. These flavors complement wild meats well, as some of the ingredients may have been a part of the animal's usual diet. Small amounts of juniper berries can be combined with other berries like mountain ash, currants, or chokecherry to zest up jellies, jams, or chutneys.

How to Preserve

Juniper-berry-infused vinegars and honeys preserve the distinct pine-rosemary aroma well. Juniper-infused honey goes well over wild salmon before baking or grilling the fillet.

Dry juniper berries whole to use in marinades and brines. Juniper, beebalm, and Douglas fir needles combine well and make a great trio of wild ingredients to have on hand for your Thanksgiving turkey or Christmas goose brine. These same three ingredients can be used to create an herb-flavored salt. Combine the fresh herbs with coarse salt and blend well with a food processor, coffee grinder, or mortar and pestle. Let the salt blend sit in a bowl or shallow pan for a few days; mix daily, until the salt and herbs are dry. Enhance the salt mix in a smoker, burning some juniper twigs as the salt cures even further. This salt can be used to flavor foods before, during, or after cooking as a finishing salt.

Future Harvests

Junipers provide a lot of food for animals during the winter months. Be mindful of where you are foraging and harvest only where trees are plentiful.

Caution

Pregnant women or people with known kidney disease should not consume juniper berries or foods that include it.

king's crown

Rhodiola integrifolia

EDIBLE shoots, leaves, flowers

King's crown is a foragable food for the mountain climber sleeping above treeline; its juicy, tart young leaves are a refreshing snack, midday or -night.

How to Identify

King's crown is a succulent in the stonecrop family. Its juicy, flattened, cauline leaves are oblong with a pointed tip. The thick leaves attach alternately to the stalk without a petiole. Flowers are small with four or five petals of a deep red-orange. They form a rounded cluster at the top of the unbranched stem. Roseroot (*Rhodiola rosea*) looks similar and is likewise foragable; it has a light pink spike of flowers, and its rootstalk has a slight rosy floral fragrance.

Where and When to Gather

Discover king's crown growing abundantly in rocky outcroppings where not many other plants would have success. This

Find king's crown growing in rocky outcroppings on mountain slopes.

The flowers of king's crown are a red-tinted burnt orange and form a rounded cluster.

succulent prefers the rocky, moist, and well-draining soils of the mountains and can be found above treeline and below, in the shade of the forest edge. Gather the young shoots before the plant has flowered in late spring. Gather the leaves and flowers throughout the summer.

How to Gather

Young shoots can be cut near the base. Cut or break off the stalk of older plants about 4 inches down, giving you some leaves and flowers.

How to Eat

King's crown can be eaten raw or cooked. Sometimes leaves gain bitterness and lose tartness after the plant has flowered, but cooking them ameliorates the bitterness. Steam the leaves, clipped tops, or young shoots, and toss them in melted beebalm-and-onion-infused butter. When car camping with the proper cooking utensils and a dozen eggs, use king's crown in frittatas or omelets. Pick apart the flowers and toss them into salads or place atop cooked dishes.

Future Harvests

In lush places below treeline, king's crown can be found growing in large stands. Above treeline it may be a different story: in places where it is not growing in large colonies, harvest only small amounts.

lamb's quarters

Chenopodium album

goosefoot

EDIBLE leaves, stems, seeds

My friend Steve made a passing remark to a visiting farmer—the bugs seemed to be feasting on the lamb's quarters that had cropped up in his garden, not the spinach. The farmer's response? "Which one do you think has more nutrients?"

Find lamb's quarters growing in thick stands, invading your vegetable garden and other disturbed soils.

Another common name for this plant, goosefoot, is a loose translation of the genus name, which itself derives from the Greek, *chenos* ("goose") and *podion* ("little foot"), in reference to the shape of the leaf.

How to Identify

Spotting lamb's quarters from a distance can be easy: plants can grow over 6 feet high (but average 4 to 5 feet) and the waxy coating on the green leaves, particularly on their undersides, makes them appear slightly gray. Leaves have the shape of a goose foot: a rounded triangle with irregular, shallow lobes or teeth. The first true leaves are opposite and covered in a gray-white, waxy coating that can be rubbed off on one's fingers. The rest of the leaves are arranged alternately along a stem that is gently grooved and sometimes tinged with red. Flowers are inconspicuous green balls; they grow in branching clusters, putting forth tiny black seeds.

Where and When to Gather

Lamb's quarters is found all over the world, predominantly in disturbed areas and inhabiting all soil types. It may be found in your garden as a nutritious invader, growing abundantly in vacant city lots, or on the side of a mountain road at 10,000 feet. The first sprouts of lamb's quarters are seen in spring, and if the garden is erupting with them, weed them out for eating. Gathering can be done until about midsummer. Then, as the ground dries up, so does the plant; however, because lamb's quarters reseeds itself so well, some young plants may reappear in the fall. Seeds can be collected from late summer through fall.

How to Gather

The abundance of this plant can make a bountiful gather easy. When the plant is young, pluck off leaves or pinch off the top of the plant. Plucking about 2 to 6 inches off the top is ideal for a tender stem. The tender stem is edible as well, and can be chopped up to go with the greens.

When gathering the seeds, first shake the tops to see if any of the seeds pop out. If some do, then they are ripe. Break off the stalk and beat the seed clusters into a bucket to get the seeds loose. Use your fingers to free any remainders on the stalk. The gathered seeds will then need to be sifted and winnowed. Don't worry about any remaining chaff; it's just extra fiber.

How to Eat

The leaves and stems (and even the small flowers) are edible raw or cooked. The leaves have a texture similar to spinach when boiled, steamed, or sautéed. The raw leaves are good but better cooked into meals. Treat lamb's quarters as wild spinach and go to town. Be creative and add it into lasagna, frittatas, or spanakopita. Seeds are edible sprouted or cooked, a bitter-tasting cousin to quinoa; they can be ground and added to baked goods and cereals, or boiled like quinoa.

How to Preserve

Make a nutrient-rich infused vinegar from the leaves, stems, and young seedheads. Leaves and tender stems can be blanched and frozen for future meals. Drying lamb's quarters and grinding it to powder makes it easy to add to future smoothies or green drinks. The seeds will keep for months if dried.

Future Harvests

Lamb's quarters is on invasive weed lists across the continent; there are no sustainability issues when it comes to harvesting it.

lilac

Syringa species

EDIBLE flowers

One of my favorite springtime activities is riding bikes through town with my family and deeply inhaling the aromatics of fragrant and—surprise!—edible lilac flowers.

How to Identify

Lilacs are not usually found in the wild, but they grow well in the Rocky Mountains as an ornamental. Most are growing on landscaped property—maybe even in your own backyard. These deciduous shrubs can grow tall if you let them, but most people keep them pruned. Lilacs host flowers ranging in color from purest white to classic shades of purple and magenta; they grow in panicles and are highly aromatic. Leaves are ovate or heart-shaped and have entire margins. The grayish brown bark is smooth in younger years and with age

Lilac's aromatic blossoms won't last long, so be sure to make use of the flowers while they are in full bloom.

begins to peel and flake in longitudinal stripes.

Where and When to Gather

Find lilacs escaping from yards or abundantly planted in a neighbor's landscape. Gather the flower clusters in spring until about the start of summer, when they start to dry and fade.

How to Gather

Clip the flower clusters first thing in the morning, while they are super fragrant. Try to harvest before the sun heats up and zaps away the delicate aromatics. Rinse off any cobwebs or bugs in a strainer.

How to Eat

While the flowers are blossoming, I make sure to have a batch of lilac water with me for every farmers' market we vend. People are shocked at what a lovely flavor the infused water is and that those are lilac blossoms floating in the water. Depending on the vessel you are infusing your lilac water in, you may want to pick apart the clusters, so they fit better. If it is a big glass container with a pour-dispensing spout, leave the lilacs in their whole clustered shape; it looks marvelous. More importantly, leaving the cluster whole prevents the flowers from separating and clogging the spout. If it is a smaller pitcher separate the small clusters from the main stalk. This will allow flowers to float in each person's drink. Use cold water and about five clusters per gallon of water—more, if you want it stronger-tasting. Infuse lilac blossoms in honey for a fragrant sweetener to add to teas and baked goods or lick straight off a spoon.

How to Preserve

Lilac cordials can be made, or simple syrups. Try infusing vodka with the sweet scent. Lilac syrup can be frozen in ice cube trays for easier use in individual drinks.

Future Harvests

Always make sure to ask before you start trimming someone's lilac bush. The flowers bloom only in spring and are highly regarded for their fragrance as well as their gorgeous look.

linden

Tilia species

basswood

EDIBLE leaves, flowers, nuts

Although linden is not native to the mountain west, it grows well as a landscape tree and is commonly planted throughout cities, the jasmine-magnolia scent of its flowers wafting through streets and neighborhoods on hot summer days. Be sure to capture it in infused honey or a simple syrup.

How to Identify

Tilias are tall (30 to 100 feet), full-looking trees, often with low branches and short trunks. Trees are densely branched and often multitrunked; trunks are straight.

The bark is gray or brown in color and can be furrowed, fissured, or even have flat ridges, depending on the species. Leaves are heart-shaped and serrated around the margins, often smooth on top with soft hair

Linden trees can be smelled long before you turn the corner and realize the entire street is lined with this beauty. Their dense, hardy flowers are filled with sweet, soft notes of jasmine and magnolia.

Fill a jar halfway with fresh plant matter such as the leaves and flowerheads of beebalm, the berries of skunkbush or smooth sumac, rose petals and -hips, cottonwood buds, or linden flowers—the list of plants you can infuse is really endless. Cover with raw local honey, and then stir the herbs to get a good coating and to release air bubbles.

Set the jar on a sunny window ledge for two to four weeks or heat in a double boiler at a very low temperature. Create a simple double boiler with a pot of water and place your jar into the water bath; honey will be infused in four to eight hours. Strain honey from herb while it is warmed. I have to be honest: some herbs I never strain—I leave them in the honey. The honeyed herb either makes it into food dishes unnoticed or gets strained with my tea. This honey will stay stable for at least a few months, shorter if the plant had a lot of water content.

on the underside. Flowers are a pale yellow with five petals and hang in clusters on a stem, from a leaf-like bract. Bracts are long and narrow and pale in color compared to the vibrant green leaves. The flower stem attaches to the center vein of the bract. Nuts are round and hard, containing two seeds.

Where and When to Gather

Linden trees are generally not found growing in the wild in the mountain west. Be leery of gathering near heavily trafficked roads, landscaped buildings, and municipal areas. Find a happy tree in the yard of someone who does not use chemicals on their lawn, and ask permission to gather there. Gather leaves in spring. Flowers begin blooming in late spring and continue into midsummer. Nuts can be gathered in late summer.

How to Gather

In spring, while the leaves are tender and small, they can be plucked from the tree; they have a slightly sweet taste. Find a tree that is loaded with highly aromatic flowers in the summer. It is very easy to pick a lot of flowers quickly from a large, old tree. Crack nuts open with your teeth to get to the small seeds inside.

How to Eat

Leaves make a nice addition to spring salads, as they have a subtle sweetness to them with a tender bite. Linden flowers have the fragrance of honeyed jasmine with a touch of magnolia. Capture their scent in simple syrup for softening summer drinks with its sweet floral taste.

How to Preserve

Linden blossoms in honey are one of my favorite ways to preserve the delicate aroma of the flowers. Drying the flowers for tea is nice, but it does not harbor all the notes. This is why I like to double up for my linden tea with dried flowers and infused honey. Make sure to store the dried herb in a sealed container.

Future Harvests

Linden flowers provide a lot of nectar for bees; watch out for these buzzing friends while you are foraging, and try not to take too much from them.

mallow

Malva neglecta
cheeseweed

EDIBLE leaves, stems, flowers, seedpods, roots

Seedpods of *Malva neglecta* look like sliced cheese wheels but taste like sweet peas.

How to Identify

Mallow has palmate leaves with a texture of soft velvet from the tiny hairs that can be found on most of the plant. Leaf margins are scalloped, which makes each leaf look ridged. Leaves have long petioles; they are all basal at first, with stem leaves occurring alternately up the flowering stalk. Flowers are white to soft pink, usually with darker pink or purple striping radiating from the flower's center to the heart-shaped tips of its petals. Seedpods are disc-shaped and look like a sliced cheese wheel.

Where and When to Gather

This introduced weed grows all over the mountain west, primarily below 8,000

Mallow will be flowering at the same time it has gone to seed. The cheese-wheel-shaped seedpods are a crisp and tasty snack.

The palmate leaves of mallow are carried on extra-long petioles.

feet. Mallow is a drought-resistant plant that does well in rocky or dry, disturbed soils. It is mostly found near places that have been frequented by people, not so common in the wilderness. Mallow leaves and stems are full of minerals, which show the efficiency of the root system for pulling them out of the soil; this also means you should not harvest near contaminated soils or old mines. Gather the basal leaves in spring, the flowers in summer, and then toward summer's end, the seedpods.

How to Gather

The whole fresh plant can be uprooted from spring through summer and is entirely edible. The seedpods are a favorite forage and can easily be gathered by plucking.

Make bundles of fresh herb for a simple way to dry and crumble the leaves. Simply clip the plant about 3 to 4 inches down along the main stalk. Always look for stems with abundant foliage. Tie the clipped ends tightly together and hang the herb bundle upside down, in a dry spot that is out of direct sunlight. In about a week, the leaves will be dry enough to crush off the stems and store in a clean jar.

How to Eat

The nutrient-rich leaves and roots of mallow are great to use as thickening agents and can be added, fresh or dried, to stews, soups, gravies, and sauces. Replace commonly cooked greens with mallow leaves, or decorate the tops of salads with the delicate flowers just before serving. Seedpods of mallow have a taste similar to peas and the slimy texture of okra; they are perfect in curries or vegetable dishes in need of more consistency. Find recipes online for making marshmallows from scratch using the boiled goo of the seedpods.

How to Preserve

Dried mallow roots and leaves are a great addition to the tea cabinet in arid climates. To take advantage of their moistening and soothing effects, always prepare the tea as a cold-water infusion, especially if you are a person who constantly battles the dryness. This could be a nice drink to have on a regular basis. Young green seedpods can be pickled and used as a caper substitute.

Future Harvests

Mallow is a hardy nonnative. There is no need to worry about harvesting the whole plant. The plant grows annually, so gathering all the seedpods for consumption will limit next year's growth. If you would like to propagate mallow, let the plant self-seed, replant seeds, or use cuttings.

mariposa lily

Calochortus species

EDIBLE flowers, bulbs

Mariposa is "butterfly" in Spanish, and a field of mariposa lilies in bloom, waving in the wind, does indeed look something like a field of hovering butterflies. Flowers are an unrivaled final touch to spring and summer dishes.

How to Identify

Mariposa lilies vary greatly in color, depending on the species or variety. Most petals of our most abundantly common species throughout the mountain west, *Calochortus gunnisonii* and *C. nuttallii* (sego lily), are primarily white or pink. Each bears a darkened band or splotches of purple or burgundy toward the flower's hairy yellow center. The three petals surround six stamens and a three-way lobed stigma; below the petals are three sepals. A single basal leaf blade extends up from the bulb in spring; later leaves are grass-like, held alternately along and clasping the slender stem.

Where and When to Gather

Mariposa lilies are found throughout mountain meadows, foothills, and aspen groves, either scarcely scattered or in widespread colonies. Flowers bloom from late spring to midsummer. Roots are best gathered during the summer monsoon season, when it is easier to dig them out of the softened ground.

How to Gather

Be thoughtful when plucking flowers. Check to make sure none of the mariposa lilies you may be encountering are on a threatened species list, and spread your harvest out through the patch. The bulbs grow deep; carefully follow the slender stems down into the earth (see caution) to be certain you are digging up the bulb of a mariposa lily. Bulbs will need to be washed and peeled of their darker outer skin to reveal the creamy white beneath.

How to Eat

Flowers can be picked and eaten raw. They are best added to salads after they have been tossed, so the gorgeous flower does not get decimated. They make the loveliest garnish to the sides of any dish. Bulbs should be enjoyed roasted with other roots, or added to soups where they can be cooked for a while. They have a rich smooth texture and a minimal flavor that blends well with most things, but they definitely become a little sweeter the longer they cook.

Mariposa lilies are one of my favorite wildflowers to admire. For this reason, I will pick only a few at a time and dish out one per person.

Future Harvests

Be gentle to this plant. Mariposa lily bulbs and flowers should be harvested only in places of abundance and in a manner that will help the plant spread: if 100 plants are within sight, take only five to 10 roots and 10 to 20 flowers. The untouched plants will have more space to grow in the now-tilled soil.

Caution

Always make a positive identification with mariposa lilies when harvesting the bulb. It is easy to snap off the slender stalk and lose the bulb in the soil, where it could be growing next to mountain death camas (*Anticlea elegans*) or meadow death camas (*Toxicoscordion venenosum*), both highly poisonous.

miner's lettuce

Claytonia perfoliata

winter purslane

EDIBLE leaves, stems, flowers

Miner's lettuce is one of the few native North American wild greens carried from this continent to Europe, where it was introduced as a tasty edible, valued for its high content of vitamin C.

How to Identify

It's always a treat to travel north and find patches of miner's lettuce in the woods of Montana or Idaho. A disc-like leaf encloses the upper stem, giving miner's lettuce a very distinctive appearance. The round leaf is actually a pair of leaves that has united around the stem, but it looks as though the stem has pierced the center of the circular leaves. Many long stems arise from the root, forming a rosette. The first true leaves are basal, long, and narrow. This plant is in the same family as purslane, with the same succulent leaves and stems. Flowers are pink or white with five petals. Each petal has a little notch at the top. The flowers look similar to those of redstem spring beauty (*Claytonia rubra*).

Where and When to Gather

Miner's lettuce thrives in areas of cool shade and dampness. It is rare to find it growing wild in Colorado or Wyoming because the land is too dry and the sun is too intense. It grows more abundantly in the woods of the Pacific Northwest, Idaho, Utah, Nevada, and southern Montana. Harvest in midsummer when leaves are biggest.

How to Gather

Pinch the stem below the biggest leaf. Leave behind a few flowering stems so they can produce seeds and renew the population. I soak the stems in a bowl of water and jostle the plant matter around to clean off any soil.

How to Eat

This crisp green is coveted in salads for its firm crunch and abundance of vitamin C. Add in chickweed, violet, and dandelion greens to give yourself the perfect spring salad to rejuvenate your sluggish winter body. Whole sprigs augment sandwiches, wraps, and spring rolls in place of bean sprouts or lettuce.

How to Preserve

Clipped miner's lettuce will stay fresh in the refrigerator rolled in a damp towel for about three to five days. This plant shrinks up considerably after blanching, so freezing it, though possible, isn't worth your precious harvest.

Miner's lettuce can be used as the base of a spring salad, being the romaine lettuce of the woods.

Future Harvests

Miner's lettuce is a rarity in the mountain west; stands are small, or few and far between. Harvest with care and always leave flowers behind to reproduce. This plant is very easy to grow and will take over an entire yard if presented the right conditions. Favoring cooler temperatures, it can do well in high mountain gardens when provided enough shade.

Mormon tea

Ephedra species

jointfir

EDIBLE stems

Mormon tea unveils a sweet, earthy flavor that is extra special when sun-brewed in a jar nestled into the desert sand.

How to Identify

Unique desert-residing shrubs, Mormon tea can be distinguished by jointed and apparently leafless green stems. These prehistoric-looking plants do in fact have leaves; however, they are small and scale-like, fused closely to the stem, and it is the junction of these leaves that gives the stems their jointed look. Mormon tea is a gymnosperm, meaning it produces spores that look more like a cone than a flower. The male and female cones of Mormon tea make the plant more similar to a pine or juniper tree than a flowering plant.

Where and When to Gather

Mormon tea can be harvested throughout the year within the desert lowlands of western Colorado, Utah, and Nevada. Even with snow covering the ground, Mormon

Mormon tea's jointed stems can be gathered any time of the year.

Find Mormon tea in desert canyons.

tea should still be visible, its green antenna stems branching toward the sky.

How to Gather

Clip sections of the jointed stems from many different shrubs, trying not to impact one area or a single plant too much.

How to Eat

A tea can be made from the jointed stems. This tea is mineral-rich and energizing, making it a great brew for the weary slot-canyon hiker. It is best infused as a sun tea. To make this, shred or cut up the jointed twigs and place them in a container or bowl full of water. Let this stand in a sunny spot for a few hours or an entire day. For an energizing tea first thing in the morning, try a moon brew, letting the herb steep in the light of a radiant moon instead. Use either hot or cold water for making tea. Mormon tea infusions can be used to replace water in baking, to add iron and other minerals to baked goods.

How to Preserve

Keep Mormon tea as whole as possible to preserve the delicate flavor. Cut the plant into small segments and store in a sealed jar. Grind or crush the herb just prior to making tea.

Future Harvests

Mormon tea should be harvested with care; trim only a few inches from each plant, spreading your harvest throughout many stands.

mountain ash

Sorbus scopulina

rowan, western mountain ash

EDIBLE fruit

Fiery reddish orange berries droop from the mountain ash tree in late summer and hang on through autumn and winter, providing a shockingly sour snack for the backcountry splitboarder on a several-hour-long hike up a valley.

How to Identify

Mountain ash is a shrub-like deciduous tree, capable of reaching moderate heights of 20 feet. Leaves are made up of nine to 12 pinnately compound leaflets. The entire leaf grows alternately along the branches. Each leaflet is lanceolate with serrated margins. The tree resembles an elder (*Sambucus*), with its cluster of white flowers and compound leaves; however, mountain ash has more leaflets than elders, and if you rub the leaves of mountain ash, they do not give off the unpleasant odor that elder leaflets do. Being a member of the rose family, the berries look like miniature apples, growing in clusters, turning from fiery orange to red when ripe.

Where and When to Gather

Find these trees at the openings of conifer forests in the foothills and mountain valleys. Berries are best gathered after the first few frosts; cold snaps set the sugars in the fruit, which softens the berries and renders them less sour. A common ornamental, European mountain ash (*Sorbus aucuparia*), can be used similarly.

How to Gather

Mountain ash berries grow in clusters, making them easy to gather quickly. Snip the clusters into a basket and pick the berries off the stems at home. When processing your harvest, discard any hard or discolored berries, along with the stems.

How to Eat

Mountain ash berries are bitter before they have been frosted over by the first winter chill, but sugar can make anything sweet, right? Wild game chutneys can be made with orange, ginger, and a blend of hawthorn, mountain ash, and juniper berries. This makes a tasty glaze for wild birds such as grouse, duck, and goose. The berries can be cooked down into a juice, for jelly or syrup. Try using in combination with crabapples, rosehips, skunkbush berries, and other wild fall fruits.

How to Preserve

Berries freeze well and can be dealt with later for processing. Mountain ash berries can be used to infuse liquors, or made into wine.

These are the fiery orange berries of mountain ash in late summer.

Future Harvests

Mountain ash trees grow plentifully where found, and harvesting berries should not pose a threat to this favorite food of the birds.

mountain candytuft

Noccaea fendleri

prairie pennycress

EDIBLE leaves, stalks, flowers, seedpods

I love picking the sweet, mustardy-flavored flowering stalks of mountain candytuft in spring. It is even better with the crispness imparted by a rainy or snowy day.

Mountain candytuft is a small plant with a spicy bite.

How to Identify

Mountain candytuft stands no taller than 6 inches, approximately. It has a rounded cluster of small white flowers. Each flower has four petals and the tetradynamous formation of stamens (four tall and two short) that mark all mustard-family plants. An unbranched stem arises from small, ovate basal leaves. The leaves along the stem are small, ovate to lanceolate with entire margins, and hug the stem closely. Seedpods are heart-shaped.

Where and When to Gather

Find mountain candytuft growing alongside dwarf bluebells, spring beauties, and violets in mountain meadows. The time to gather is spring when the plant has flowered, making it a little more of a substantial harvest.

How to Gather

Pick mountain candytuft at the base of the stalk. The whole plant can be utilized. Leaves and flowers are usually too small to separate from the stalk.

How to Eat

Mountain candytuft is such a small plant, I do not find it worth cooking; I have always just enjoyed it raw. I take the flowering or seeded stalk and chop it up a little, adding it to salads, or add the flowering stalks to sandwiches and wraps as a sort of sprout substitute.

Future Harvests

Mountain candytuft grows abundantly throughout the sloping hills of the mountain west. It would be hard to overharvest it, but—as always—take only as much as you need.

mountain gooseberry

Ribes montigenum

gooseberry currant, alpine prickly currant

EDIBLE fruit

The fruit of mountain gooseberry may look a little intimidating, covered as it is in soft bristles, but don't hesitate to try the sweet red berries.

How to Identify

Mountain gooseberry is a small shrub of the alpine. It has prickly stems and branches, along with fine bristles on the outer skin of the berries. Leaves are sticky and fuzzy. The berries are red and smaller than other gooseberries. Flowers are pinkish orange and saucer-shaped, not as tubular as other *Ribes* flowers. A similar-looking plant is prickly currant (*R. lacustre*); its leaves are smooth, and its deep purple or black berries are also very good.

Where and When to Gather

Mountain gooseberries are found throughout the Rocky Mountains, mostly above 6,000 feet, preferring dry to moist mountain soil. Find the low-spreading bush under the canopy of spruce forests. Berries start to ripen in summer and can be gathered into early fall.

How to Gather

The small fruits are easiest to collect if you simply snip branches that are dangling a constellation of berries and process when you get home.

How to Eat

Enjoy the tart berries fresh while hiking in the mountains. When cooked down, the pulpy juice can be used for syrups, jellies, or sorbets. Use whole berries for pies, compotes, and puddings.

How to Preserve

Like other gooseberries they can be mashed and made into fruit leathers. The fruits can be dehydrated and combined into trail mixes and granolas. Clusters of berries can be frozen whole.

Future Harvests

Picking the berries has no bearing on the future harvest of this plant, but the wildlife may depend on it for food, so always leave some berries behind. Seeds, seedlings, and cuttings propagate well when planted in rich soils.

Don't mind the tiny, soft bristles on the outer red skin of mountain gooseberries.

mountain parsley

Cymopterus lemmonii

Indian parsnip, spring parsley

EDIBLE leaves, roots

These parsley-flavored leaves are one of the first wild culinary herbs of spring in mountain meadows.

Mountain parsley can be found blooming in early summer with tender leaves. Use the leaves as a garnish, just as you would traditional parsley.

How to Identify

Leaves are finely dissected, fern-like, often with a reddish tint to the petiole, and grow from the base of the stem. Flowers are bright yellow or sometimes reddish purple umbels. They grow on stalks that can reach up to 2 feet in height. Mountain parsley is the most abundant yellow-flowering umbel in the Colorado and Utah mountains. Look to the seeds for the indicating difference between this species, which has a poorly developed winged seed and noticeable dorsal ribs, and *Lomatium* species, which have flattened and winged seeds.

Where and When to Gather

Find mountain parsley in mountain valleys and on rocky slopesides and sunny forest floors. Leaves will start showing up in early spring in cool subalpine meadows. It is easy to spot the small yellow umbels against the rocky soil and under the pines and aspens. Gather the leaves through the summer. Roots are best harvested in spring and fall.

How to Gather

Some plants do not produce a lot of leaves; for this reason, take only one leaf per plant. Gather roots only if you are in a place where plants are truly numerous, and even then take only one or two to sample their parsnip-like flavor.

How to Eat

The taproot is edible as well as the leaves. Use the leaves as a spice and flavoring. Mince them to bring a little zest to a salad or salsa, or to garnish a culinary work of art. The root can be added to soups and stews.

How to Preserve

Dry leaves, crumble them, and store them in a spice jar. Add a pinch here and there to sauces, soups, or roasts. Make infused butters and oils with fresh leaves, or add to vinegars.

Future Harvests

Stick to taking just a few leaves here and there, and only if the plants are abundant.

Caution

These plants are in the family Apiaceae and should be identified with 110% certainty. Be clear on what both water hemlock (*Cicuta* species) and poison hemlock (*Conium maculatum*) look like, starting with their white-flowered umbels.

mulberry

Morus species

leaves, fruit

I am always thrilled to find a mulberry tree in city limits or, even better, in an abandoned lot, where I can keep returning all summer long for more of the sweet and juicy berries.

How to Identify

Mulberry trees have low, long wavering branches that radiate out in all directions from the central trunk, making it a rather easy tree from which to access fruit. The trees stand between 30 and 60 feet tall, though they are often much smaller. The bark is gray-brown and can have a copper hue; it is smooth while young and becomes rough with vertical furrows as it ages. Leaves vary greatly on a single tree. Some are heart-shaped with serrations; others can be lobed, looking like a mitten, or have multiple notches. The leaves are arranged

Wait for white mulberries (*Morus alba*) to turn red before picking, as that is when they are fully ripe and taste best.

Mulberry leaves are all different, with mismatched lobes and irregular toothed margins.

alternately along the branches. White mulberry (*Morus alba*) leaves are glossy; those of red mulberries (*M. rubra*) are not. This difference in appearance is the distinguishing factor.

Berries start out white or green, turning red and staying light in color (*Morus alba*) or turning a deep purple-black (*M. rubra*). The tree will be full of many different-colored berries, as they don't all ripen at the same time.

Where and When to Gather

Morus alba is an introduced species from Asia, and *M. rubra* is native to the eastern part of North America. Mulberry trees are often found with true wild abandon. I usually spot them in alleyways, parks, or at the edges of old pasturelands. Gather the young spring leaves for tea. Find the berries ripening in late spring and through to the height of the summer.

How to Gather

Gather individual leaves, taking only a few per branch. Plucking berries is time-consuming but fun if you are out only for a feral snack. If you really want to get the berries down, lay a sheet or blanket below the tree and shake the branches. The ripe berries will drop.

How to Eat

Fruits from mulberry trees have a taste unlike any cultivated berry. They are dense, with a mild tart sweetness all their own. Mulberries are the perfect not-too-sweet-fruit and as one of the first of the summer, why not try making ice cream?

How to Preserve

Berries can be made into jam or jelly for future toast slathering; try mixing in wild apples, serviceberries, or hawthorn berries to add natural pectin to help set up the consistency. They freeze well if laid flat on a tray first. Mulberries also dehydrate well and can then be blended into granolas and trail mixes or placed atop yogurt. The dehydrated berries are better to add into baked goods; sometimes fresh mulberries hold too much juice.

Future Harvests

White mulberry is considered invasive in the eastern United States. Gathering the berries from either white or red mulberry trees will not affect either's survival.

New Mexico locust

Robinia neomexicana

EDIBLE flowers

The pink flowers of New Mexico locust, the only locust native to the mountain west, taste like a sweet pea with an added soft floral fragrance.

How to Identify

New Mexico locust is a deciduous tree or shrub. Trees are thin-trunked and are usually found growing in thickets. Light pink or magenta flowers grow in clusters among the pinnately compound leaves. Leaves are long and have many rounded leaflets, each tipped with a tiny bristle.

The clustered pink flowers of our native New Mexico locust appear in high summer. Note the tiny bristle on the tip of each leaflet.

New Mexico locust blossoms smell heavenly but stick to eating only them, and only a few.

Each leaf node has a set of ½-inch or smaller spines. The long seedpod is flattened and covered in glandular hairs.

Where and When to Gather

Find New Mexico locust growing wild in southern Colorado and Utah. It can be found along riverbanks and in canyons and mixed conifer forests, growing among scrub oak and juniper. Find it planted as a landscape tree in towns above 7,000 feet, as it withstands extreme temperatures very well. Clusters of rosy pink flowers hang from New Mexico locust in the summer months. Gather on a dry day while they are highly fragrant.

Black locust (*Robinia pseudoacacia*) is not native to the mountain west; however, it can be found at lower elevations (3,000 to 5,000 feet) and is often planted in yards and along street boulevards. It has white flowers that can be used the same way as New Mexico locust.

How to Gather

Flowers can be plucked from the hanging clusters or you can snip down the whole bunch. Pick the flowers off of the green stem to eat. All other parts of New Mexico locust are said to be toxic if ingested.

How to Eat

Pluck just the flower without the stem straight from the tree and eat. Garnish dishes with this beautiful edible flower. Add the flowers to salads or use them to top sandwiches and tacos. Dip in egg and flour to create a battered flower that fries up well in oil. Try making simple syrup, but do so on very low heat as the heat can destroy most of the aromas. The sweet aromatic flavors can be captured and frozen in ice cream by infusing the cream with the flowers first.

How to Preserve

Try freezing whole clusters of flowers to use later. Flowers can be infused into alcohol for creating a floral-tasting cocktail.

Future Harvests

Picking the flowers will do no harm to New Mexico locust.

Caution

These trees are in the pea family (Fabaceae), which has many toxic members. Be cautious with both trees, eating only small quantities raw at a time. Avoid leaves, stems, bark, roots, and seeds, which are said to be toxic.

nodding onion

Allium cernuum

EDIBLE leaves, stalks, flowers, bulbs

Nodding onion is easy to find through most of the summer, when it is in bloom, and will instantly make any camping trip cuisine ten times better.

How to Identify

Onions always smell like onions. If you crush any part of this plant, you will notice the familiar scent. This allium puts forth a delicate, tall, smooth, rounded stalk that dangles a mass of lightly scented whitish pink flowers. The clusters look as though all flowers are nodding to you while passing them by. The flower stem (peduncle) falls over with the blossoms, so there is always a bend at the top of the stalk. Bulbs are teardrop-shaped with small rootlets growing out of the rounded base. Flat grass-like leaves come up from the single pink-skinned bulb. No leaves are found along the flower stem. *Allium textile*, *A. geyeri*, and many other species of wild onion can also be used.

Flowers, growing in sagebrush swales, look like nodding fireworks.

Wild-spiced salts

Use fresh herbs to infuse salts; their moisture will be wicked away into the salt crystals, infusing them with the herbs aromatics. Mince herbs finely, and mix them with coarsely ground salt. If you have a food processor, you can grind the herbs and salt to blend together. Lay the mixture on splatter screens or trays, or even a bowl could work if you stir it a few times a day. The wild-spiced salt will be infused in roughly three to four days.

To enhance the salts even more, use a smoker. It provides a smoky aroma that pairs well with conifer tips, juniper, beebalm, mountain parsley, and more. It also allows your herbs to infuse the salt faster. Place in a charcoal or gas smoker for 12 hours on a splatter screen. Different tree species will provide unique flavors and smoke; try mesquite, cherry, alder, or apple—even lilac. Use ground seeds of stinging nettle and mustard seeds at the end for their nutrients and flavor.

Use for finishing salts, seasoning fish, or as a brine, marinade, or dressing ingredient. Replace your everyday table salt with something from the woodlands. Store your salts in a glass jar for best preservation.

Where and When to Gather

Nodding onion can be found all over the mountain west, from the lowlands to the highlands, and in the land between; it is primarily found in Colorado, Wyoming, Montana, and north into Canada, and the eastern sides of Idaho and Utah, as it favors high open meadows, rocky terrain, and sagebrush country, where it gets adequate sunlight. Nodding onions are easiest to find when in bloom and best to gather while the root is still delicious, in midsummer. If you wait until fall to harvest, all the sugar is concentrated back in the root, and it is much more savory. Since the leaves and flowers are most likely gone at this point, you could find a suitable place to harvest in the summer, and mark it with a rock cairn, if you'd prefer your bulbs savory.

How to Gather

Nodding onion can grow heavily in an area or be very sparse. Gathering the root unfortunately kills the whole plant when harvesting, so tread lightly and take only a small amount from substantial stands. If you are in a questionable place, take only a few leaves and flowers. Bulbs grow fairly shallow and can be dug up with a sturdy stick.

How to Eat

I like to use the entire plant when I am making chili. First, chop up the stalk and bulb to use in place of a domestic onion. Mince the leaves and flowers to sprinkle on after you have ladled the chili into bowls. Nodding onion can be used in any dish as an onion substitute, raw or cooked. It

Bulbs are easily dug out, but do this only when you are among many other nodding onions.

always amazes me how long the taste of onion lingers in my mouth after eating a few flowers or leaves, so take this into consideration before sharing a tent.

How to Preserve

Onion can be pickled, infused in butter or oils, or incorporated into vinegar infusions. Do try wild-spiced salts with nodding onions.

Future Harvests

Never take all the leaves or flowers from one plant, as this compromises its growth and reproduction. If it is the bulb you are after, please be very conscious of where you are harvesting; this native plant is abundant in some parts of the Rocky Mountains and not seen much in others. Take only a few bulbs at a time; they go a long way.

Caution

Be careful not to confuse this plant with meadow death camas (*Toxicoscordion venenosum*) and mountain death camas (*Anticlea elegans*), both extremely toxic and inedible plants that could be mistaken for the shoots and leaves of nodding onion. Once these poisonous plants have bloomed, there is no problem distinguishing them from nodding onion: the flowering stalks of both grow upward in a raceme. In addition, both will lack the onion scent when their leaves are bruised, and their roots have black scales on them and are oval-shaped.

Western blue flag (*Iris missouriensis*) is another look-alike plant you should not consume; it too has grass-like leaves that can be mistaken for young allium leaves. Once again, they will lack the onion scent, and the flowers are blue irises.

The scent of onion can linger on your fingertips from one plant to the next, so do be very careful in your identifications.

northern bedstraw

Galium boreale

EDIBLE leaves, stalks, flowers, seeds

Northern bedstraw grows amply in the Rocky Mountains. Leaves and flowers can be used for a sweet mineral-rich infusion.

The whorled leaves and square stems of northern bedstraw make it easy to identify even out of flower.

How to Identify

Northern bedstraw has small skinny leaves, growing in whorls of four at each node along the stalk; they are toothless but have fine hairs along their edges. Stems are smooth and square, becoming branched only toward the top, where flower clusters form. Flowers are white with four white petals and pointed tips.

Where and When to Gather

Northern bedstraw can be found on mountain slopes, throughout conifer and aspen forests, or in moist meadows with partial shade. Gather the young stalks before the flowers bud or bloom; flowers and leaves when they are present; seeds in the fall.

How to Gather

Simply clip off the part of the plant you are interested in. Again, the young tips of the plant are best before the plant blooms and goes to seed. Gather seeds by using your hand to rake them into a paper bag.

How to Eat

Northern bedstraw is not the most flavorful plant, but it has a ton of nutritional value. The young stalks can be chopped and eaten raw or cooked. Leaves and flowers can be brewed into a subtly sweet infusion. Blend the leaves and flowers with other nutritionally dense herbs such as stinging nettle, red clover, and alfalfa for an extra-nourishing brew. This strong infusion can be added to soup broths or used to cook rice and pasta. This is a great way to add a boost of essential minerals and vitamins to anyone's diet.

How to Preserve

Dry and crumble leaves and flowers for making tea. Northern bedstraw is a distant relative of coffee, and its seeds can be collected, dried, roasted, and ground for a similar taste. After roasting but before grinding, store seeds in a sealed container. Grind the seeds in a coffee grinder just before making tea.

Future Harvests

Northern bedstraw is a hardy perennial that grows in colonies through a horizontal root system and also spreads by seed. Your foraging will have no impact on it, particularly if you harvest only the stalks.

orache

Atriplex species
saltbush, shadscale
EDIBLE leaves, seeds

A dash of salt is instantly added to your favorite dish when orache is part of the mix.

How to Identify

Orache looks similar to lamb's quarters but can be differentiated by its leaves. The leaves of orache are more triangular and shaped like an arrowhead, with a downward-pointing base, whereas the leaf base of lamb's quarters points up. Both plants share the gritty gray substance that makes their green leaves look slightly steel blue, but the mildly salty taste of orache is not shared by lamb's quarters. Orache leaves are toothed or wavy, growing opposite along the shoot when young and turning alternate as the stem grow taller. Plants are 4 feet or more in height, and as they mature, leaves can grow quite large. Flowers are small, green, and clumped together at the tips of branches or where the leaves join the stem.

Orache has a downward-pointing leaf base, and mature leaves can span from 1 to 6 inches.

Gather the tops of orache or its leaves while they are still vibrant and crisp.

How to Gather

Pinch off the shoots and the tops of the plant. Be sparing for the plant's sake and take only a few leaves from each plant. In fall, seeds can easily be gathered by using your hand to rake them into a paper bag. Winnow away any chaff.

How to Eat

The tender shoots and tops can be enjoyed as a salad green or cooked. They are a great addition either way, offering their subtle salty flavor and texture. Be sure to taste a dish with orache before adding any additional salt. As orache ages, the leaves firm up a bit, so use it as a green to accompany any cooked dish. It is similar to spinach but with a salty twist. Seeds can be used as thickeners for soups and stews after they are both roasted and ground up. Try sprouting them for crisp micro-greens.

How to Preserve

Greens can be blanched and frozen for future use. Leaves can also be dried and crumbled for a slightly salty seasoning.

Future Harvests

Taking a few leaves from each plant and stripping some seedheads will not endanger the future of these plants.

Where and When to Gather

Orache is a fairly common plant in cities, gardens, and disturbed areas of the mountain west. In fact, our region is home to a few dozen species of *Atriplex*. Some are herbaceous perennials; others are shrubby and have a woody base (the latter mostly grow in the desert lowlands). All the many species of *Atriplex* are edible and can be used in a similar way. Find orache growing in sunny pastures and meadows or even along shaded riverbanks or at the edge of forest. Plants prefer moist to dry, salty or alkaline soil. Gather shoots and the tops of the plant in late spring and early summer. Leaves can be gathered well into late summer. Seeds can be gathered in autumn.

Oregon grape

Mahonia repens
holly grape, barberry

EDIBLE fruit

These small blue berries pack a powerful punch of tartness—nothing a little sugar can't tame, though.

How to Identify

Oregon grape is a bit of a misleading name for a plant that grows so low to the ground with no vines attached. The compound leaves are evergreen and reminiscent of holly leaves; they are deep green, waxy-feeling, and thick with jagged edges that can be sharp to the touch. The small flowers are bright yellow and carried in a dense raceme. Berries start out green but turn a deep purplish blue when fully ripe. When the inner root bark is scratched, it will show bright yellow.

The berries are ripe when they are chalky blue outside and seriously sour and juicy inside.

Oregon grape has jagged evergreen leaves and clusters of yellow flowers.

Where and When to Gather

You will find Oregon grape growing in pine forests, rocky slopes, and sagebrush lowlands. Berries are ripe in late summer and can still be found as the snow blankets the ground. Some foragers claim the berries are best if found after the first frost. Be advised, the birds are on it, so timing is everything.

How to Gather

Clusters of berries can be clipped off, or picked individually. Some berries are sweeter than others; tasting a berry from each plant can be helpful in being selective about how tart you want your harvest to be. Avoid berries that have any green on them; they can cause stomach irritation.

How to Eat

I do eat the berries right off the plant, but only a few, as the flavor sends a jolt through the mouth that forces me into submission. Some berries are more delicious than others, holding a sweeter, sour-grape flavor, while others are intensely tart and astringent. Each berry contains one seed, which can be removed with a food mill or strainer when processing.

How to Preserve

Berries can be frozen fresh for later processing and be made into jellies, syrups, juice, wine, and fruit leathers.

Future Harvests

Leave some berries behind for the birds, so they can continue to spread this creeping evergreen throughout our mountain places.

ox-eye daisy

Leucanthemum vulgare

EDIBLE leaves, flower buds, flowers

Pluck the closed flower buds and pickle them for a caper-like wild delicacy.

How to Identify

Ox-eye daisies can be found in more places than people would like, as they spread quickly both by seed and vegetatively, through their shallow rhizomatous root system. A thick rosette of deeply colored green leaves forms first, before the flowering stalks of ox-eye daisies are sent up. Smaller leaves grow alternately up the flowering stalk. Leaves are widest at the tips, narrowing to long, flattened petioles. The leaf margins are jagged, irregularly toothed, or lobed. The composite daisy has white ray flowers radiating from the bright yellow center, which is made up of tiny, densely packed disk flowers.

Young leaves taste of carrot with a hint of celery.

My favorite parts are the unopened flower buds and leaves picked from the stalk or base of plant.

Where and When to Gather

The plant is a major noxious weed in the mountain west and is heavily sprayed in areas where control is attempted, so be very careful in your choice of where to gather. Native grasslands, meadows, riverbanks, and pastures are the best places to start looking for this daisy. It likes disturbed soils that are well drained in full to partial sun. Gather its leaves, flower buds, and flowers from spring until late summer.

How to Gather

Basal leaves are larger than the leaves growing up the stalk, but both are tasty, with great salad-green texture. Since this is such an invasive weed, taking the majority of the leaves from a rosette is not a problem. Gather the leaves from the stalk by sliding your thumb and index finger down the stalk to release the leaves into a basket.

How to Eat

The young leaves blend perfectly in spring salads, amplifying the flavor of the mix with their celery or carrot-like notes. Toss in some of the budding flowers, or better yet, pickle them first and bring them along into the backcountry while foraging. Use the pickled buds and vinegar for dressing wild salad greens. Use full-blown flowers to garnish dishes, or dip them in a tempura batter for an appetizing fried treat.

Future Harvests

Ox-eye daisy is considered a noxious weed in many parts of the mountain west because of how densely it spreads, decreasing the populations of native plants. This is one plant that can tolerate overharvesting. If it seems like it is crowding out other plants, pull up the plant by its root when gathering the leaves.

Caution

Ox-eye daisy is in the Asteraceae, and some people may have allergic reactions to this plant family.

You will be surprised how flavorsome this common weed is.

pennycress
Thlaspi arvense
fanweed

EDIBLE leaves, flowers, seedpods

Nibble a fresh seedpod of pennycress and be inspired to create your own wild mustard sauce.

How to Identify

You have probably recognized this plant once it has gone to seed with its light green, semi-swollen, circular seedpod.

As a kid we used to collect the seeds and use them as our own currency. Four-petaled white flowers adorn the top of pennycress at the same time the lower

The edible disc-like silicles, or seedpods, of pennycress.

You will hardly find pennycress standing alone, which makes gathering a breeze.

seedpods are swelling. Flowers bloom on short stems that stick away from the stalk, looking like a rounded cluster toward the top of the plant. Leaves are lanceolate and alternate, hugging the stem closely.

Where and When to Gather

Pennycress can be found high up in the mountains or along your backyard alley-way. Look to the weed havens and dis-turbed soils that get full to partial sun. Be sure to gather in a place that is free of spraying; avoid gathering from the sides of roads and parks. Gathering can be done from spring to fall, starting with the leaves or flowers buds and ending with the dried seedpods.

How to Gather

Grab a whole stalk; not only the green seedpods but also the rest of the plant can be eaten. Trim off leaves and flowers for salads. Once the plant has begun to die back, you can run your hands through the dried plant to collect the seedpods.

How to Eat

Pop green seedpods in your mouth right off the plant for a spicy treat, or add a handful to salads. Fresh seedpods can be blended into vinaigrettes for dressings and marinades.

A little can go a long way in cooked dishes like stews and stir-fries. Add a bit at a time, tasting often until you get the desired flavor. Dried or fresh seedpods can be ground into wild mustard. Use the seeds of other mustard-family plants, such as pepperweed and shepherd's purse, to round out the flavor.

How to Preserve

Dried seedpods can be stored in the spice cabinet for future use in flavoring dishes. The dried seeds can be a nice spice added to pickled and fermented goods. Use fresh seedpods to infuse olive or coconut oils, and drizzle these multipurpose oils over salads all winter.

Future Harvests

Another mustard invader—eat your weeds! Eating the seeds should have no impact on this plant's survival.

pepperweed

Lepidium species

peppergrass

EDIBLE leaves, seedpods, roots

Pepperweed is a mustard-family plant found throughout the mountain west. Chances are you walk past this plant daily, taking no notice of it as a source of black-peppery spice.

How to Identify

Basal leaves of pepperweed are often buried under the snow of winter. These young leaves are jagged and usually lobed, widening out from the base. The raceme of white or yellow (*Lepidium flavum*) flowers makes pepperweed look like a bottlebrush. Leaves on the flowering stalk are lanceolate

Clasping pepperweed (*Lepidium perfoliatum*) produces small round spicy silicles, or seedpods, by mid-spring.

Whatever the species, the silicles of pepperweed are easy to strip from the stalks by pulling upward with your fingers along the stalks.

and toothed, growing alternately up the stem. Seedpods, or silicles, are green while young and turn tan as they dry out; they are round and somewhat flat. Besides *L. perfoliatum*, the most common species in the mountain west are *L. densiflorum*, *L. montanum*, and *L. virginicum*.

Whore and When to Gather

Pepperweed is found everywhere in our region; it will show up in pruned lawns or sprouting through a crack in the pavement. The best places to find it are disturbed soils, old pasturelands, and sunny fields. Young basal leaves can be gathered throughout the year. Seedpods are best while still somewhat green, as they lose flavor the longer they dry out.

How to Gather

Snip or break off the seeded stalk. Roots are best gathered along with the green silicles.

How to Eat

Young leaves bring a peppery bite to spring salads, salsas, or pestos. Peppery-tasting green seedpods add pronounced spice in cooking, pickling, or making condiments like stone ground mustard. Blend and grind young wild mustard seeds—pepperweed, pennycress, shepherd's purse—together with spices, honey, and vinegar for a delicious spread. Roots can be used as a substitute for horseradish when ground with a little vinegar and salt.

Future Harvests

Forage to your heart's content. This plant spreads prolifically; it can become your front lawn if you don't manage it.

pine

Pinus species

EDIBLE needles, resin, pollen, nuts

I make it a point to swerve my way through pines while snowboarding, inhaling their warming resins on a sunny day. It often smells of men's cologne or aftershave. I always stop and snag a lodgepole pine needle to softly chew in between my teeth for the pleasant citrus flavor.

How to Identify

Often we look at a conifer and automatically call it a pine, when in fact it may be an entirely different genus, such as fir (*Abies*), spruce (*Picea*), or Douglas fir (*Pseudotsuga*). The needles of many *Pinus* species are much longer than those of other conifers, making the tree branches look tufted. Pine needles come in bundled sets of two (lodgepole pine), three (ponderosa pine), or five, as in limber pine (*P. flexilis*) and whitebark pine (*P. albicaulis*).

A cluster of male cones on lodgepole pine (*Pinus contorta*) at almost the perfect stage for harvesting pollen.

Processing pine pollen

In the spring, you will notice the male cones loaded in yellow pollen. Ponderosa and lodgepole pines are my favorites and can harbor the most pollen. First you need to know when the pollen should be there, and this happens between April and July. You may first notice the pollen on cars around the neighborhood; this is the opportune time to get out there before it quickly blows away.

Pine pollen can be collected while cones are on the tree or collected off the tree at home. In order to collect pine pollen directly from the trees, have a paper bag, plastic bag, or deep bowl on hand. Bending a branch so that its cone clusters are inside the bag or bowl, shake the branch vigorously, releasing the pollen into the collection container. It will take the shaking of many branches from numerous trees to collect a substantial amount.

To process at home, trim off the cone clusters and collect them in a plastic bag or large bowl to maintain all the pollen. Let the cones sit and dry out in a large bowl at home for a day or two. Then shake the clusters into a bowl, releasing the pollen. Store this nutritious powerhouse in the freezer for maximum freshness.

The male cones (technically catkins) are soft, shed pollen in the spring, and lengthen before falling off the tree. Female cones are woody and scaly, with pine nuts nestled in between the scales. The nuts are covered by a hard protective shell, or are flattened, with a wing for wind dispersal of the tiny nut. Some pines, such as the lodgepole, have female cones that remain tightly closed for years, opening only in the event of a forest fire; the heat of the fire will open up these so-called fire cones, releasing seeds to help reseed forests after a burn.

Where and When to Gather

Pines are found in most places of the mountain west. Ponderosas are the most widespread, occurring at lower elevations and in drier climates, including Nevada and Utah. Lodgepoles can be found throughout, while whitebark pines are found primarily in the northern Rockies, intertwined with limber pines. These two pines grow in the higher elevations, with the whitebark pine growing at elevations close to 12,000 feet in some places. Gather male cones in spring, when they are short, in tight clusters, and full of the powdery yellow pollen; touch the cone cluster, and if powder puffs off into the air, they are ready. Resins are easily gathered in the spring or fall, when it is dripping from wounds in the trees. Gather female cones, for their nuts, in the fall. Needles can be gathered year-round.

The cones of the ponderosa pine (*Pinus ponderosa*) can be a good source of the aromatic resin.

How to Gather

Clusters of male cones can be clipped with pruners. A glass jar works best to store the sticky resin. Look for freshly trimmed branches, scarred trees, or cones that are oozing the clear resin. Gather female cones from the forest floor. Needles can be gently tugged from the branches. Spread out your harvest between many trees. The younger trees, which will be easier to access, should be picked from the least, as they are trying to grow and mature.

How to Eat

Pine pollen can be added into any food combination. Try blending pollen into smoothies, sprinkling over cooked dishes, or mixing into batter for baking or frying. Simple syrups of needles and resin can be made for creating sparkling pine sodas and cocktails.

How to Preserve

Pine nuts can be roasted, shelled, and frozen for the longest shelf life. Infuse oils, honey, and vinegar with the needles and resin of pine for future cooking endeavors that could use a lemony-pine twist. Needles can be chopped and dried for future tisanes. Store pine pollen in the freezer after processing your harvest; it is best stored in a sealed glass container.

Future Harvests

Harvest only from trees that are not under stress from pine beetle. This invader has killed many pines in the mountain west and has also led to a lower production of cones in some species. Since pine nuts can be a substantial source of food for many bears, birds, and other critters, they are best left untouched in strained areas.

pineapple weed

Matricaria discoidea
disc mayweed
EDIBLE leaves, flowers

Crushing the small flowering heads of pineapple weed disperses a sweet tropical scent high in the Rockies. Capture the taste of this scent in tea.

How to Identify

Pineapple weed is a low-growing weed that's easy to miss even when it's right in front of you. But step on it, and it announces its presence. When crushed, the cone-shaped flowers disperse an aroma of fresh pineapple and sweet chamomile. Flowers look like little green-yellow buttons, consisting of small tightly packed disc flowers. Pineapple weed lacks the

Collect the yellow flowerheads for their sweetly tropical, pineapple-like flavor.

white ray flowers of German chamomile (*Matricaria recutita*) and other species in the genus. Flat, feathery, sweet-smelling leaves are pinnately dissected and grow alternately along the flowering stalks. Many leafy, flowering stalks arise from the root, making this stubby plant look full and bushy.

Where and When to Gather

You can find pineapple weed just about anywhere throughout the mountain west, but it may not draw any attention to itself because it grows so small and close to the ground. Flowers are best harvested in the full heat of summer, as they are most aromatic at this time.

How to Gather

Use a small pair of scissors or your pincer fingers to gather the leaves and flowers of pineapple weed. There is no need to wash the plant matter if you harvest from a grassy spot; however, a bowl of water can be used to soak and rinse trimmings that are too sandy.

How to Eat

The delicate leaves can be strewn into salads for a hint of sweetness. Flowers are best brewed fresh with cold water to make a refreshing iced tea. Add in other aromatic herbs such as wild mint or cota for a very pleasing summer infusion.

How to Preserve

Leaves and flowers can be dried on a screen or in the dehydrator for a short time. Store in a sealed glass jar to preserve the sweet aromas.

Future Harvests

Pineapple weed is abundant and happy in the west. Trimming leaves and flowers from the plant will not put a damper on its future, as it reproduces and spreads easily.

Caution

Pineapple weed is in the Asteraceae, and some people may have allergic reactions to this plant family.

piñon

Pinus species

pinyon

EDIBLE needles, resin, nuts

Many people go through life loving the nutty aroma of pine nuts, having no idea that they are from the cones of a piñon.

How to Identify

Two species of piñon grow in the mountain west, *Pinus edulis* (two-needle piñon) and *P. monophylla* (single-leaf piñon). Both are short and bushy pine trees. They do not grow in dense forests because they need space to send enormously long roots horizontally and deep into the ground to gather enough water during drought. *Pinus edulis* has two needles in each fascicle (the cup that holds the needles together); *P. monophylla* is unique among pine species,

Piñons are a smaller conifer, with one of the biggest pine nuts to offer.

This young resinous piñon cone holds the sweet buttery golden morsels of prized nutmeat.

with only one needle per fascicle. Both species have rounded resinous pine cones that are stout, measuring 1–2½ inches in length and roughly an inch in diameter. Inside are brown egg-shaped nuts and their golden nutmeat, known as pine nuts.

Where and When to Gather

In the mountain west, trees are primarily found in Utah, Nevada, and Colorado. Find two-needle piñon in Colorado, Utah, and parts of southern Wyoming, and single-leaf piñon in Nevada, Utah, and a small southern zone of Idaho. Piñons grow in the canyon lands or rocky dry soils along with juniper and ponderosa pines, at 4,000 to 9,000 feet in elevation.

Gather resin in winter and needles all year long. For nuts, the best time is September through November. Timing matters immensely because the nuts are dispersed from the cones and quickly picked up or plucked out by birds: earlier in the season brings more abundance. One year could be a bumper crop, and the next you may not find many—or any—nuts in the cones.

How to Gather

Pull the needles gently off the branches without protection, but throw on some rubber gloves or disposable latex gloves if you want your hands to be functional after harvesting the cones. The delicious resin is intensely sticky. It is quite disappointing to crack open a pine nut and find it empty. This means the nut was self-pollinated. It is easy to distinguish these rapscallions by

Piñon nuts prior to being shelled.

the color of the shell: lightly colored shells are the fool's gold, and the darker brown shells hold the coveted meat.

How to Eat

I wish pine nuts were easier to harvest: they are pretty pricey at the store, but they can accompany so many different dishes! Roasted pine nuts in the shell can be eaten like sunflower seeds. You crack them open with your teeth and spit out the shell. Roasting the seeds, shelled or unshelled, releases the oils from the meat and really brings out the flavor. A single nut contains up to 20 calories, made up of mostly fat and protein. Make a wild trail mix of dried currants, pine nuts, and dehydrated wild strawberries. Infused olive oil from tree resins and needles can be made. Add in ground roasted pine nuts, and you have a wonderful oil for dipping bread or any culinary use.

How to Preserve

Roasting extends the life of the nut for storage in the refrigerator or freezer. Shelled pine nuts sealed in an airtight container and stored in the refrigerator can last for a month or two, while frozen nuts will last about nine months. Unshelled pine nuts seem to have a longer shelf life than those shelled if they are stored in a dry and refrigerated place.

Future Harvests

It is really hard to gather a lot of nuts, and it's rare that the seeds germinate on their own.

plantain

Plantago species

EDIBLE leaves, seeds

Use ground plantain seeds in combination with other gluten-free flours for a better consistency when baking. Their gelatinous components help bind other ingredients together.

How to Identify

Ovate or lanceolate leaves of plantain grow in a dense basal rosette. Leaves have parallel veins that attach to thick stems. If you pull the leaves apart or break the stem, you will see that the veins are very stringy, like celery. Plantain hugs the ground, forming a mat of leaves around the leafless flowering spikes. The thin flowering spike hosts tiny white flowers that turn into brown seedpods. English plantain (*Plantago lanceolata*) and broadleaf plantain (*P. major*) can be used interchangeably.

Where and When to Gather

Plantain seeds have been spread far and wide by the movement of people and other animals. The mucilaginous seeds easily

The ovate leaves of broadleaf plantain (*Plantago major*) are arranged as a basal rosette that hugs the ground closely.

Plantain leaves are thick, which makes them suitable for battering and frying.

plump up and stick to fabrics, furs, feet, hooves, and wheels, which carry them long distances. Plantain can be found high up mountain trails past 10,000 feet and low in the tropics. Find the best leaves in spring or early summer. Gather seeds in late summer.

How to Gather

Gather the choice young leaves by plucking them at the base of the thick petiole. As plantain ages, the leaves turn tougher and more bitter. Seeds can be gathered by trimming off the seeded stalk. Take the stalk and winnow the seeds off, letting seeds fall into a bowl. Remove all the husks and store the seeds in an airtight container.

How to Eat

Plantain leaves are tender and slightly tart, not bitter, while they are young. Use the leaves for salads or minced on fish tacos. Younger and older leaves can be used in soups or stews for their nutritional abundance of vitamin A and calcium. Plantain seeds can be added to gluten-free baked goods, for binding ingredients together. The seeds also work well in smoothies.

How to Preserve

Dry the leaves and crumble them to store for tea blending or future culinary use. Store them in a glass airtight container. Fresh plantain leaves can be blanched and frozen for future recipes. Seeds can also be dried and stored for later use.

Future Harvests

Plantains have no trouble reseeding themselves. Little harm is done by taking seeds or leaves from these lovely little weeds.

Caution

Plantain seeds promote bowel movements, so do not take in conjunction with other laxatives.

prickly pear
Opuntia species

EDIBLE pads, flower buds, flowers, fruit

Prickly pears vary greatly throughout our region. The best have big juicy fruit with a crimson, seed-filled, fleshy center that smacks of sweet melon.

How to Identify

About 200 *Opuntia* species exist worldwide, many of them throughout North America. Here in the Rockies and mountain west deserts, they hybridize with each other, making identification a little tricky sometimes. Chief characteristics are their flat pads (nopales) and brightly colored fruit. Both the pads and "pears" are covered in spines and glochids (tiny bristly spines with barbed tips—very unpleasant to the fingers). Flowers are showy and range in color from yellow to pink.

If you can get past all the spines, the flowers and even their buds are edible as well.

The crimson, juicy, seed-filled fruit of prickly pear.

Where and When to Gather

Prickly pears are found in the desert lowlands and dry, usually south-facing slopes of the mountain west, in between mountain ranges and among the sagebrush. Pads can be gathered most of the year, when there is plenty of moisture; during dry spells, the pads shrivel up and are not succulent. Gather flower buds and flowers in spring. The pears can be collected in late summer and fall. In colder climates, plants tend to produce small inedible fruits.

How to Gather

Opuntia pads can be gathered by clipping a pad free of the entire plant. The spines and glochids can then be burned, cut out, or scrubbed away with water. Once the spines are removed, the skin can be left on or cut off before consuming. An easier way to harvest pads is to leave them attached to the whole cactus while you slice the pad in half. This way you can easily scrape each side of the pad and get a good amount of the mucilaginous center. Once you have used this method, cut off the remaining mangled pad; otherwise, you leave the cactus open and vulnerable to pest infestation or infection.

Flowers (yes, even they and their buds have prickles to avoid) and pears can be picked with a bare hand, but gloves or tongs make it an easier and less glochid-filled experience.

How to Eat

First come the flower buds, which can be a tasty trailside nibble; be careful of the tiny spines at their tips. Once bloomed, the flowers can be quite satisfying on a hot day if you are mindful of the sharp spine at the tip of each petal. Pears have super-fine glochid patches on the skin and some long spines. The best way to remove these is to singe them off with a flame; alternatively, use a stiff brush and scrub them in a bucket or a sink full of water. Cutting the pear in half shows the marvelous ruby glow of the fleshy fruit, loaded with black seeds. There are a ton of seeds for the little amount of fruit inside, but scooping the seeds out and scraping the sides of the fruit will give you something to work with. Mash the seeds and flesh through a strainer to yield delicious raw juice.

Nopales are famously grilled in the Southwest, used as a meat replacement in tacos, taking on the flavors of the spices used. Add diced chunks raw to salads for a tart addition. The pads can also be boiled for roughly five minutes before pan frying; this removes a lot of the slime and firms them up a bit.

How to Preserve

Try infusing the pears in vinegar for a prickly pear vinaigrette. The fruit pulp can be added to jellies or dehydrated into fruit leather. Its juice can be simmered with sugar and made into simple syrup. Infuse into alcohol to add a southwestern flair to martinis or margaritas.

The best way to start preservation of the pads is to slice them up and boil for about a minute to remove the mucilaginous texture. Sliced nopales can also be marinated and dehydrated for a beef-jerky-style snack. Or the slices can be laid out flat on a tray, frozen, and placed into freezer bags for easy retrieval. Pickling and canning the slices is another option.

Future Harvests

Never take the whole cactus; it takes them many years to reach maturity. Leave some pears behind for seed distribution and if harvesting the flowers, take them from several cacti; do not strip any one cactus of all its buds or flowers. If you happen to take off a pad and are not using it, place it back in the soil and it will set roots.

purslane

Portulaca oleracea

verdolagas, pigweed

EDIBLE leaves, stems, flowers, seeds

I told my in-laws that this trespasser of their garden bed is edible. Now they weed for the slightly lemony-tasting succulent greens of purslane.

The succulent leaves and stems of purslane form a matted ground cover.

How to Identify

Look low to the ground, for a sprawling, flat-leaved, succulent green plant that has a smooth, thick, red stem, ovate leaves, and tiny yellow flowers that have five petals. The leaves rarely exceed an inch in length, and the plant itself doesn't stand more than an inch or so tall. Seeds are small and black.

Where and When to Gather

Purslane grows all over North America in disturbed soils, preferring a warm climate. The best place to find purslane is in a garden bed, and yet it probably was not included there intentionally. City parks tend to have rogue patches sprawling through the grass lawns. Farmers are now cultivating it and adding it to your farmers' market salad mix. You can find this succulent thriving in the heat of the summer, withstanding droughts and scorching sun.

How to Gather

Trim or snap off the trailing stems of the plant a few inches from where they emerge from the ground. The leaves, stems, flowers, and seeds are all edible. To make cleaning easy, soak the purslane in a water bath to loosen up any soil that is clinging to the plant.

How to Eat

Raw purslane is slightly mucilaginous, giving salads a sour, crisp bite. Tapenades, salsas, and other spreads are brightened by its lemony taste. It also chops up nicely to add to stir-fries or stews, as a thickening agent. This nutrient-rich succulent is packed full of omega-3 fatty acids and can be a summertime substitute for fish oils. I find purslane nice to chew on while gardening on a hot day; it brings a moistening tang to my taste buds.

How to Preserve

Purslane is a succulent and therefore not a plant for drying, and its mucilaginous quality, when cooked, makes it difficult to use for canning and not so great for freezing. Its fat stems, however, are a prime candidate for pickling.

Future Harvests

Purslane grows pretty abundantly and overharvesting should not be an issue. Leave a few stems behind if you want to reseed the area.

raspberry

Rubus idaeus
red raspberry

EDIBLE leaves, flowers, fruit

It is such a treat that this fruit grows high in the mountains among the jagged rocks. There is nothing better than stumbling upon a ripe raspberry patch while hiking in late summer's heat.

How to Identify

Raspberries that grow wild are smaller than cultivated varieties but more mouth-watering. Depending on elevation and climate, raspberry bushes can be quite large, maxing out at about 8 feet, or be very dwarf; on high mountain cliffs, they may reach only a foot in height. Leaves are

The berries are plump and red when ripe. Size can vary greatly, depending on elevation. The lower the elevation, the bigger the berries.

Find raspberry bushes growing close to water—or far from it, high on a craggy mountainside.

ovate, deeply veined, and jagged around the edges; they grow alternately up the spiny stems, in a compound formation of three to five leaflets. They are deep green, sometimes having a reddish tint around the edges; their undersides are lighter, with soft white fuzz. Flowers are small, delicate, and white, with five tiny petals. The fruits are called berries for simplicity's sake, but in reality each "berry" is made up of many minute drupelets, each drupelet containing an individual seed. When you chew a berry, you will notice all the small seeds released onto your tongue.

Where and When to Gather

Raspberries are found all over the mountain west, in yards, in woods, near water, and on the craggy hillsides of the mountains, in partial shade or sunny places. Gather leaves and flowers in early summer, the berries as they appear.

How to Gather

Leaves for tea are best gathered when the plant is in flower, and including the edible flowers only adds to the eventual taste. Wearing gloves can be helpful when gathering because of the prickly stems. Dry the leaves and flowers on a screen or in paper bags. Once everything is dried you can easily crush the leaves in your hand, or the leaves could be chopped before being dried. Berries are easiest picked one by one and placed into a sturdy container that won't smash the delicate fruit.

The best time to gather the leaves to dry for tea is when raspberry is flowering.

How to Eat

Obviously we know how to eat the berries, and it is really hard to bring any home most times. When you do manage to collect a bounteous amount of berries, indulge in making pie, ice cream, sorbet, and syrup for sodas, or try creating a vinaigrette. The vinaigrette can include berries and leaves. Infuse the leaves and berries in vinegar for about a week, strain, and add honey for a nutrient- and mineral-rich vinaigrette. Leaves make a super nutrient-dense infusion, rich in minerals and vitamin C. For the strongest tea, take a handful of leaves and place them into a quart-size jar or French press. Pour freshly boiled water over the herb and let this steep over night, consuming it the next day as a nourishing brew or simply infuse the herb in hot water for 20 minutes.

How to Preserve

Raspberry jam is a must-have for every pantry stock. Berries can be frozen whole; for an easy way to keep them from forming one massive clump, see sidebar on page 68. Raspberry juice or puree can be frozen too; ice cube trays are a great way to form small bricks for single use.

Future Harvests

Harvest berry, leaf, or flower—just do not take all the plant parts from one bush.

red clover

Trifolium pratense

EDIBLE leaves, flowers

Red clover provides us with a bountiful source of nutrition. Pick out the little flowers from the clover blossom and suck out the honey-like nectar—no wonder cows love it!

How to Identify

Fields are dotted with the pinkish red, puffed flowerhead of red clover. The blooms consist of many small, tubular flowers that each hold a drop of nectar. Leaves are soft and have three leaflets per stem, looking like a shamrock, with each leaflet graced by a light chevron-shaped mark. Stems are hairy, and the leaves are arranged alternately along it.

Where and When to Gather

The best place to find red clover is at the forest's edge, or in a meadow that is free of heavy cattle grazing and far from pesticide-laden farms. Because red clover

Gather the flowers and leaves early in the morning, before the rains come, if you want them to dry properly at home. Never store them before drying, as they retain a lot of moisture and can easily mold.

Every flowerhead consists of many tiny flowers, and each contains a drop of sweet nectar.

readily absorbs minerals from the soil, stay clear of polluted soils, and do not harvest near old tailing piles from miners. The blush-red blossoms are a part of late spring's overwhelming floral celebration and can be found through to the end of summer.

How to Gather
Pick a basketful of red clover blossoms and leaves on a sunny, dry day; this ensures the blossoms can dry mold-free. Use your hands to pluck flowerheads, or bring a pair of scissors. Go for vibrant red flowers, not the ones turning brown, and pick the greenest leaves.

How to Eat
A nutrient-dense plant that doesn't come with much flavor makes red clover a great secret ingredient for the meek or picky eater. Steeping the herb in freshly boiled water for at least 30 minutes can make a strong infusion of the leaves and flowers; this infusion can then be used to soak legumes or cook rice and pasta, ensuring the added minerals of calcium, magnesium, and potassium. Flowers and leaves can be added to fresh salads, but they are a little dry and best eaten when they are young. Instead, make a salad dressing from vinegar that has been infused with the flowers and leaves of red clover. This will be chock-full of all the minerals and vitamins red clover has to offer. The flowerheads can be cooked; they impart a slight flavor of sweet pea when added to frittatas, stir-fries, or steamed mixed veggies.

How to Preserve
Flowerheads and leaves can be dried for infusions. Make sure blossoms are not damp or browned when harvested to maintain freshness and prevent molding. Lay the flowerheads out on a mesh screen immediately after harvesting. Let the herb dry away from direct sunlight.

Future Harvests
Red clover is mostly known for being a weed, and a really hard one to eradicate, so don't worry about taking the flowering tops. Just make sure you are gathering in a clean, non-sprayed area, and stay away from soils polluted with nitrates, heavy metals, or pesticides.

salsify

Tragopogon species

oyster plant, goat's beard

EDIBLE shoots, leaves, flower buds, roots

Salsify is cultivated in other parts of the world for its root, which has a pleasing parsnip-like flavor.

How to Identify

Salsify is reminiscent of dandelion (milky sap and a similar flower with identical yellow hue), the local exception being purple salsify (*Tragopogon porrifolius*), whose flowers are a dull purple; however, salsify has long basal leaves that are narrow, not toothed, and its shorter, slender leaves grow alternately up the stalk. What's more, the flower of salsify is set in a large green bract whose pointed tips extend beyond the blossom; in the heat of the day and at night, the bract closes the flower into a pointed bud. One last similarity between dandelion and salsify is the puffed white seedhead: salsify has a much larger fluff of pappus-bearing achenes. Taproots look like a scrappy carrot and are creamy white or beige with thick skin.

Extended green floral bracts and long, grass-like leaves set salsify apart from dandelion and other look-alike edibles such as sow thistle and wild lettuce.

The young grassy-looking leaves and stem of salsify.

Where and When to Gather
Find salsify in meadows enjoying direct sunlight, or rocky and disturbed soils below 9,000 feet. Salsify is a biennial; second-year plants put up a flowering stalk, and the young shoots can be collected. Shoots, leaves, and roots are all best in spring, before the plant has flowered; after flowering, roots turn tough and fibrous. The flower buds can be enjoyed as a wild food in summer.

How to Gather
To collect the young shoots, pinch the base of the stem. Roots need to be dug with a shovel or sturdy digging stick. They hold a lot of dirt; scrub well and peel before using. Make sure to harvest the root crown and basal leaves of young plants. Buds of flowers can be plucked off the stem.

How to Eat
In Europe, unlike here, *Tragopogon porrifolius* is highly regarded for its roots, which once cooked taste like oyster. Roots, to me, have a sweet, almost parsnip-like flavor. They do well boiled or roasted with other tubers like rutabaga and turnips. Young shoots, leaves, and flower buds are mildly bitter and can be mixed into salads with other wild greens. Later-season foliage can be incorporated into cooked dishes to tame the bitterness.

How to Preserve
Salsify greens and roots can be blanched and frozen. Chop roots before drying and, to carry more flavor, roast the root before storing. Use the dehydrated root in autumn root vegetable purees or soups.

Future Harvests
The wind-dispersed seeds of salsify are carried far and wide. Regarded as an invasive weed brought over with European crops, this plant cannot be overharvested.

Caution
Salsify is in the Asteraceae, and some people may have allergic reactions to this plant family.

scrub oak

Quercus gambelii
Gambel's scrub oak

EDIBLE nuts

Most acorns need to be leached or cooked to remove the tannic acid, but scrub oak has acorns that are sweet enough to be eaten after roasting, or some even raw.

How to Identify

Scrub oak is a native shrubby tree, averaging heights of 10 to 30 feet, growing much taller than that if it has an adequate water source. Leaves have the common trait of family members in the Fagaceae, with anywhere from seven to 11 deep lobes; they are a deep green and so shiny they look waxy. Scrub oak forests are impassably scraggily, and the hillsides they cover are lit up each autumn with their red fall color. The acorns are under an inch in size

Gather scrub oak acorns straight off the tree, for once the acorns fall, they are quickly taken by critters. Look for the ones that are outgrowing their shell.

Leaching acorns

Many acorns are astringently bitter and full of tannins. Leaching draws the tannins out. There are two methods of leaching, one using hot water, the other using cold water.

In the hot-water method, whole acorns are thrown into a pot of water. Make sure to have about a 1:3 ratio of acorns to water. Bring the water to just a boil and then strain. Taste the acorns, and if they still taste bitter, repeat the heating process until you have no more bitter-tasting tannins.

Cold leaching takes a little more time but is well worth it. Cold-leached acorns maintain a starch that acts like a gluten binder but have no gluten at all. This is useful when you want to bake with acorn flour and also preserves the sweet nutty flavors. Add your freshly shucked or roasted acorns to a food processor or blender and cover with enough water to make a puree. Blend very well and add this mixture to a much larger jar that will accommodate the addition of a similar volume of water. You want roughly a 1:1 ratio of ground acorns to water in your large jar. Shake well and place jar in refrigerator.

The following day, strain this incipient acorn flour through super-fine cheesecloth. Taste the flour; if it is still bitter, repeat this method for a few days (up to a week if you are using a species other than *Quercus gambelii*). After the final strain, you will need to really wring out your acorn flour in the cheesecloth. Do this over a bowl, and collect the water, with its fat and starch remnants.

Let this fatty, starchy water settle for an hour. Then pour off the top watery portion and add the remaining fat and starch to your flour mixture. Flatten out the flour mixture for drying. Use a dehydrator at the lowest temperature, or place the mixture outside, out of the sun's light. Flip the flattened mixture every few hours while it's drying to ensure it dries completely before storage.

with a scaly cap that covers about a third of the nut. Acorns start out green and turn brown with age and ripeness.

Where and When to Gather

Scrub oaks grow on dry hillsides in the southwestern portion of our region, in large stands among sagebrush, serviceberries, and prickly pears. September can be a prime month for gathering acorns, depending on your elevation and location. Don't get discouraged—not every year is a big acorn year, and the bounty varies from stand to stand.

How to Gather

Acorns can be gathered while still green, as long as they seem large enough. Do not

Find stands of scrub oak in the rolling hills of the mountain west, primarily in southern Wyoming and dominating Utah, western Colorado, and southern Nevada.

wait too long, as animals anticipate their readiness. Some scrub oaks provide a ton of acorns, while others may not fruit much. You can gather acorns and keep them in the shell for a few months once dried. Spread them out on a flat surface somewhere safe from critters. Keep them in a single layer, and rotate every day or so to prevent mold while they dry. If you decide you do not want to wait, which is completely understandable, crack them open fresh. The best way to crack open an acorn is to remove its cap, position the acorn with that flat side down, and gently strike the pointed end with a hammer. Peel away the shell (though I use my teeth quite often). Once the nutmeat is out of the shell, toss it directly into a container of water to prevent oxidation of the skin color.

Some acorns may provide a lovely home for grubs. An easy way to fish out the occupied nuts is to clean all your acorns first in a big bucket of water. The acorns that sink are keepers; the floaters might have an insect inside.

How to Eat

If acorns taste bitter when you nibble one raw, then they need to be leached prior to using. Leaching will make them into the most palatable and delicious nut possible. I have found that shelled and roasted acorns of this species are flat-out amazing and not very bitter at all, almost tasting like a hazelnut or chestnut; however, if you have neighborhood oak trees, they can be put to similar uses—they will just need a little more leaching than scrub oak acorns.

Scrub oak does not produce the biggest acorns, but flavor trumps size.

Acorns can be roasted in the shell. If the acorn is still green, you can wait for the acorn shell to brown first, but it isn't really necessary. Roasting makes the shell a little more brittle and easier to crack. Acorns can replace chestnuts in a turkey stuffing or be used among other flours in baking. Use the flour to thicken gravies or create a roux from acorn butter and the flour. Roasted acorns can be made into tea, or salted and nibbled. Dry or fresh, roast the acorns first before grinding them into flour. Use a coffee grinder to create a fine powder; use a sifter and then repeat a grind on the chunkier pieces for an excellent baking ingredient.

How to Preserve

Acorn flour is something sacred. Keep it stored in the refrigerator or freezer to keep it from going rancid.

Fresh-roasted acorns can be chopped up and added to butter that has been gently heated for 15 minutes (be careful to melt the butter, not burn it); use the acorn butter for baking, cooking, slathering, dipping, or drinking. Yes, try a dollop in coffee or tea, because it is outstanding. Acorn butter needs to be refrigerated, or better yet, freeze it and save for springtime consumption, when there are no acorns in sight.

Future Harvest

Scrub oak primarily spreads through its root system, so overharvesting is not a danger.

serviceberry

Amelanchier species

saskatoon, juneberry, shadbush, sarvis

EDIBLE fruit

Looking similar to and tasting almost like a blueberry—but with an air of almond—serviceberries turn from green to red or a deep blue-purple when ripe.

How to Identify

Serviceberry is a small tree or shrub reaching only 20 feet in height. The bark is smooth and grayish purple. Star-like flowers blossom before the leaves fully show, forming clusters. Each flower has five slender white petals. Leaves are ovate, jagged around the margin of the leaf tip, and smooth around the base. Berries start out green and don't all ripen at the same time. Some will be red when ripe, while others are a ripe deep royal blue or purple. All berries have a crown at the tip, just like blueberries. The crown is found only on edible berries.

Where and When to Gather

In the wild, serviceberries can be found among junipers, scrub oaks, and cotton-woods. The shrubby trees are fairly

Serviceberry is a thornless rose-family shrub with slender petals of five.

The last ripe serviceberries for the season are found in late August on top of a mountain pass.

abundant throughout the Rocky Mountains below 9,000 feet. Berries tend to go unnoticed by the passerby and ripen midsummer. Serviceberry is also seen in landscapes around town; it makes a beautiful flowering ornamental in spring and brings a good bounty of fruit come summer.

How to Gather

Taste a few berries from surrounding trees. Some fruits remain somewhat mealy and not so great-tasting, even when ripe. Make sure to pick fully ripened berries for the best taste. Berries can be picked or shaken into a basket.

How to Eat

Serviceberries are some of the best trail food around, because they have higher amounts of protein, fat, and fiber when compared to other wild berries. Once berries are ripened, serviceberries are flat-out delicious. Bake berries into muffins and pies or add a handful to pancake batter. Berry juices can be concentrated into simple syrups for cocktail-blending or sorbet-concocting.

How to Preserve

Whipping up a batch of jam is necessary if you desire to harbor that sweet almond-blueberry flavor. Berries can be dehydrated whole or processed into fruit leather. Whole berries can be frozen; lay them in a single layer on a tray to keep them from clumping together. Frozen berries can be added to milkshakes and smoothies.

Future Harvests

Gathering the berries from this tree will do no harm. Cuttings and bare-root transplants propagate well, if you'd like to bring this multipurpose beauty home.

sheep sorrel

Rumex acetosella

EDIBLE leaves

Munching on the leaves of sheep sorrel while hiking is a refreshingly sour experience, sending the taste of green apple to the palate.

Sheep sorrel's long stalks with tiny red and yellow flowers are usually noticed before the succulent, tart, basal leaves.

Leaves are biggest (though that is a very relative description) before there is a flower stalk.

How to Identify

The leaves of sheep sorrel are arrowhead-shaped with small fins at the base of most leaves; they are fairly small but form abundant bright green rosettes before the plant sends up its flowering stalk. With the fire-colored red and yellow inflorescence present, the plant becomes more noticeable. Flowers are very small, but in a field of sheep sorrel they set it ablaze, making it easy to see and identify the plants.

Where and When to Gather

This nonnative Eurasian introduction is all over the mountain west at varying elevation, preferring poor, disturbed soils with high acidity and low nitrogen. Sheep sorrel can be found in sunny fields and pasturelands, along roadsides, and in clearings from forest fires or logging, but it tolerates and will inhabit riparian areas, dry mountain slopes, and the shade of conifer and aspen forests. Leaves are best gathered in the spring and early summer; however, leaves can be gathered from the bolted flowering stalks through the summer and into fall. In some places you can find sheep sorrel leaves most of the year.

How to Gather

The leaves are small, but in a saturated area one can gather a fair amount quickly. Young leaves are the most tender and flavorful. Grab onto a bunch and twist to break them from the stem.

How to Eat

A great quencher of thirst while hiking in the mountains, sheep sorrel leaves pucker the mouth and help to create saliva. Mix into salads for a decadently textured leaf that has the tang of green apple. Add to baked goods for a subtle lemony taste that accompanies other fruits well. Use to garnish soups and sauces or as a main ingredient (but see caution).

How to Preserve

Sheep sorrel does not hold its flavor well when dried. Extractions can be made from the leaves with alcohol macerations or vinegar infusions. If trying to preserve the leaves for future recipes, lightly sauté the leaves first in butter or oil before freezing.

Future Harvests

It is considered an invasive weed in half the continent, so I am pretty sure you are not a threat to its existence. The entire plant can be eaten. If being considerate to the plant's life cycle, take only a few leaves from each plant.

Caution

Use in moderation, as the plant is high in oxalates, which, if consumed in large quantities, can cause gastric upset. Individuals who have a history of kidney stones should take the most precaution with consumption quantity.

shepherd's purse

Capsella bursa-pastoris

shepherd's heart

EDIBLE leaves, flowers, seedpods

Shepherd's purse, one of the first spicy greens of spring, is there under the snow, waiting for the first melt.

How to Identify

Shepherd's purse has distinct basal leaves that have jagged teeth pointing outward and upward, not downward like the dandelion. Basal leaves are generally between 2 and 4 inches long and form a rosette around the thin flowering stalk. Some small-toothed leaves may be seen

Basal leaves are heavily lobed, while leaves along the stalk are lanceolate or oblong in shape.

Notice the heart-shaped seedpods of shepherd's purse.

gathered in late winter or early spring. The seeds of the next generation germinate in the cool nights of autumn, so fresh, young green leaves can be found again each fall.

How to Gather
Harvest the leaves right away in the spring before the plant sends up a flowering stalk; this is when they are most tender and full. Shepherd's purse will be in flower and seed by the first days of spring in lower elevations and will run its course by early summer when the days really begin to heat up.

How to Eat
Taste the greens before harvesting a bunch, as sometimes I come across greens that are very mild in taste. Young leaves, flowers, and seeds can be a nice addition to early spring salads, giving a nice mustard spice. Use sparingly in any dish: it can be a bit overpowering, especially when cooked. Try using some of the seeds for making ground wild mustard. Blend into a wild pesto with chickweed and stinging nettle tops.

How to Preserve
The leaves and seeds can be dried for future use, but both tend to lose the spicy flavor the longer they are kept.

Future Harvests
No worries. Shepherd's purse is an invasive edible that will always cover ground in the mountain west.

clasping the stalk alternately; these are lanceolate or oblong. Flowers, small with four white petals, are clustered tightly at first and then later elongate alternately along the stalk as the plant goes to seed. The seedpods are what give shepherd's purse its name: they resemble a heart-shaped pouch.

Where and When to Gather
Shepherd's purse is an invasive weed that can be found in full to partial sun, taking up space in disturbed soils. Find it in parks, along trails, or in abandoned lots. The basal rosette of leaves waits beneath the snow cover; once the snow melts, shepherd's purse can be spotted and

showy milkweed

Asclepias speciosa

EDIBLE shoots, flower buds, flowers, seedpods

Showy milkweed earns its name from its dazzling and aromatic pink-starburst blooms. Tender young seedpods take on the flavors you cook with and are an exotic addition to stir-fries.

How to Identify

There are many species in the genus; this entry refers specifically to *Asclepias speciosa*, as that is the most abundant milkweed of the mountain west, standing sturdy along most of our highways. With the exception of the flowers, showy milkweed is covered in fine hairs. The greenish red, hollow stalk is straight and hardy, growing 2 to 4 feet tall. Leaves are glossy and have a thick midvein with a creamy pink hue. Flower buds are round and tightly clustered together; each bursts open into an intricate pink star of a flower, carrying a sweet scent. Seedpods are bright green with a "bumpy" outer skin. Flat

Utilize the flower buds while they are tightly clustered or pick the blossomed showy flowers.

Get to the young seedpods of showy milkweed while they are only a few inches long.

white seeds attached to fine silky hairs fill the pod while it is young. As the pods age, the seeds dry out and turn brown, and the silk gets tougher, making it inedible. The skin can still be cooked and eaten after you scoop the insides out.

Where and When to Gather

The best spot to locate milkweed is away from the road, where the sun shines bright and the soil is undisturbed. Gather shoots of the plant in mid- to late spring, when they are under a foot tall. Flower buds can be collected in early summer; while some plants may be blooming, others will just be budding. Collect the pods in late summer while no more than 3 inches long and while seeds are still white.

How to Gather

Snap off the shoots when they are no more than a foot tall and still tender. Collect the budding flowerheads when they are still green; think of them as mock broccoli heads. Do take a peek for holes in the buds before harvesting, as monarch caterpillars find this a nice spot to nest. The pods can be pinched off; pick the smaller, younger and tender ones.

How to Eat

Boil shoots for about 10 minutes, strain, and rinse—once: many foraging authors remark that the shoots are bitter and need multiple changes of water, but I have not found this to be the case. Treat shoots like asparagus by adding some warmed butter and lemon. Flower buds can be steamed, boiled, or sautéed as a tasty side dish; try dipping them in an egg batter and making fritters. Capture the aroma of freshly bloomed flowers in simple syrups, teas, and infused honey. The young seedpods can be cooked into any dish, battered and fried, sautéed, or boiled. Again, they are best while only a few inches long; if you harvest them larger than that, you may want to remove the inner seeds and silk, as they toughen with age.

How to Preserve

Buds can be picked off individually and pickled for a caper-like garnish. Seedpods and shoots can be parboiled and frozen for later use in dishes.

Future Harvests

Unfortunately monarch butterflies are at risk from the eradication of milkweeds across the continent. They depend on this plant for larval food. So I say spread the milkweed fluff when you find a pod that is too old to eat.

Caution

Excessive consumption of this plant raw may cause indigestion. Also, when harvesting young shoots of milkweed, be aware that at this stage there is a poisonous look-alike, dogbane (*Apocynum cannabinum*). They can be distinguished from one another with a few simple identifiers. First, milkweed has a hollow stalk with the same thickness throughout; dogbane has a solid stalk that gets skinnier toward the tip. Second, milkweed leaves are fuzzy, thicker, and tend to get smaller in size the farther up the stalk they grow; dogbane has smooth, thin leaves that remain about the same size up the stalk. Both plants have milky sap, but milkweed seems to always have more.

skunkbush

Rhus trilobata

lemonade sumac, squawberry, three-leafed sumac

`EDIBLE` fruit

Sniffing the leaves of this plant may make you wonder why you'd ever sample the fruit, but you will be glad you did when you taste this tart lemonade-berry.

How to Identify

Skunkbush leaves look like miniature oak leaves, shiny but having only three lobes; when rubbed, they emit a sweet skunky odor, hence the common name. Fall foliage color is a vivid red. Berries are technically drupes, containing only one seed each. They turn bright red when ripe and are coated with a super-sour oily resin.

Where and When to Gather

Skunkbush can be found among service-berries, scrub oaks, and sagebrush in rocky soil. Berries start ripening in July; prime

Without knowing it you will be engulfed in a skunkbush stand, reaching for the reddest berries, which always seem to be in the middle of the next bush.

Berries are covered in a waxy coating that is intensely sour and tart. Lick your fingers in between picking berry clusters to taste the resin for yourself.

gathering is when the berries are bright red and glistening with the sticky resin. Gathering can continue on some bushes until the leaves are as red as the berries. Bushes that receive more water or are in the shade tend to retain berries the longest.

How to Gather

Clip off bunches of berries or grab handfuls of berries from the bush. Their sour resin will coat your fingers; I can never hold back licking my fingers while collecting the drupes.

How to Eat

What this drupe lacks in juiciness it makes up for in intensity of flavor. They are tempting right off the bush—so tart, they taste like man-made candy. One drupe is plenty to suck on in order to have a full lip-puckering experience. At home I take the berries and garble through them to pick out the stems, the leaves, and any not-so-good-looking ones. Then I place a bunch in cold water to make a pink lemonade–like drink. Make sure to mash up the berries a bit to release the flavor. Infuse berries for a few hours before straining. You could add a sweetener and a citrus wedge if you like, serve chilled. This goes really well with fresh muddled mint or prickly pear syrup.

How to Preserve

The small clusters can be frozen while fresh. Berries can be left on the stem or cleared off before storage in a freezer bag. Pink lemonade ice cubes can be made for future beverages or cocktails. Dry the berries for tea consumption. They make a great iced tea and blend well with other herbs for a tart addition. Dried berries can also be ground up to be added to the spice collection. Sumac is a staple in Middle Eastern cuisine, often as a component of the spice blend za'atar. Sprinkle it over salads, chicken, or fish for a fresh, sharp flavor.

Future Harvests

Skunkbush is pretty abundant where it grows, and harvesting the berries is not a threat, as the plant spreads by sending out underground runners.

Caution

If you have a known allergy to poison ivy, mangos, or cashews, then you may want to avoid this plant, as it is in the same family, Anacardiaceae. Poison sumac has white berries, not red.

smooth sumac

Rhus glabra

EDIBLE fruit

Spired clusters of red berries are fun for the kids to pick apart and make pink lemonade, especially in our not-so-tropical region.

How to Identify

Smooth sumac is far less common in the wild than its sibling skunkbush (*Rhus trilobata*); it is more often found as a tree-like ornamental shrub in western towns, forming thickets, with plants averaging 7 to 9 feet in height. Its berries and twigs have a waxy coating, whereas those of staghorn sumac (*R. typhina*), another close relative, are covered with velvet-like hairs. The flowers of smooth sumac are cream- or green-colored, packed tightly in a spire that turns into maroon, semi-flat berries (technically drupes, as

Smooth sumac berries starting to ripen and turn a deep shade of red.

Staghorn sumac looks very similar to smooth sumac but differs by having hairy berries and twigs.

each berry has only one seed). Leaves are pinnate with nine or more leaflets. Each leaflet is serrated around the margin.

Where and When to Gather

You'll probably have better luck finding this species around the neighborhood; in the wild, look for it at lower elevations in the foothills. Gather the clusters in summer and fall when the berries are still sticky; as time goes on and rain showers rev up, the oils get washed away, leaving the fruit not as flavorful.

How to Gather

Clip off entire red spires loaded with berries. Clusters can be rinsed if they are cobwebby or full of debris, but this can decrease flavor. It's better to pick away the unwanted.

How to Eat

Berries yield a juice that tastes like pink lemonade; reductions and syrups can be made for a tangy addition to dishes and drinks. Cooking the berries can release a little more flavor, but you lose some of the health benefits, such as all the vitamin C. When making juice, pour cold water over the clusters and work all the berries off the stem with your fingers. Crushing and mashing them brings out more flavor. Let the berries infuse for a few hours and strain them out. After your infusion is strained, you could add sweetener, mint, or a citrus wedge.

How to Preserve

Freeze whole clusters of berries while they are fresh and still sticky. Another option is to freeze or dry the berries for tea. They add a really nice citrus tone to tea blends. The cold-water infusion, after straining, can be placed into ice cube trays for individual servings. The berries can also be dried out for a must-have spice in the cupboard; it can be combined with sesame seeds, beebalm, and salt to make a wild rendition of za'atar, a Middle Eastern spice blend.

Future Harvests

Clipping off the cluster of berries does no harm to this plant. Smooth sumac propagates through its underground runners, which is why you rarely see just one shrub.

Caution

If you have a known allergy to poison ivy, mangos, or cashews, then you may want to avoid this plant, as it is in the same family, Anacardiaceae. Poison sumac has white berries, not red.

sow thistle

Sonchus species

shoots, flower buds, leaves

A noxious weed in many parts of the mountain west, sow thistle provides mildly bitter-tasting young leaves that rival the dandelion.

How to Identify

Sow thistle does indeed have yellow dandelion-like flowers; however, you will find the alternate leaves growing up its stem are somewhat prickly at the edges and hug closely to the stalk. Even basal leaves can be distinguished from dandelion greens by the spiky outer edge. When stems and leaves are torn, they exude a milky latex sap. Sow thistle is also commonly confused with wild lettuce, another bitter edible weed with milky latex, but

Sow thistle looks something like a giant, leggy version of dandelion when in bloom.

Unopened flower buds are nice as a salad topping, pickled or raw.

they too are easily distinguished: wild lettuce has spiked hairs along the midrib underneath the leaf. Seedheads of sow thistle are white and fluffy.

Where and When to Gather

A renegade in most gardens, sow thistle can be found around the borders of parks and trails. Stick to gathering all parts of the plant while it is still young and not bloomed, in early summer.

How to Gather

Gather young stalks before they become branched, basal leaves, and tightly closed flower buds. Unopened flower buds can be plucked off the branched stems. Peel stalks before or after cooking.

How to Eat

Young shoots, after being peeled, are quite enjoyable in buttered vegetable medleys or stir-fries. Shoots can also be peeled raw, chopped, and combined with young leaves to add a mildly bitter essence to summer salads. Younger leaves of sow thistle, lamb's quarters, and orache can be sautéed with lemon and garlic for a wildly pleasing side dish.

How to Preserve

The young flower buds can be pickled and used as a garnish, similar to capers.

Future Harvests

Some *Sonchus* species are on noxious weed lists. These are quick-growing weeds that spread easily by seed.

Caution

Sow thistle is in the Asteraceae, and some people may have allergic reactions to this plant family.

spring beauty

Claytonia lanceolata

lanceleaf spring beauty

EDIBLE leaves, stems, flowers, roots

Stems and leaves add a succulent citrus flavor to springtime culinary creations.

How to Identify

Spring beauty is a small plant with succulent pink or red stems. Flowers are a pinkish white with five petals and only two stamens. Usually only a single pair of green lanceolate leaves accompanies the flowering stem. When more stems come from one tuber, this signifies that the plant is several years old and should have a decent-sized root. Roots are round and starchy, much like a miniature potato. They will vary in size depending on the richness of soil they inhabit. Tubers are rarely found larger than an inch.

Where and When to Gather

Spring beauties come with the season's name and are one of the first plants to crop

The roots of spring beauty can vary in size and can be hard to uncover. It is common that the stalk breaks off before you dig deep enough to get out the tasty little roots.

A perfect springtime scene: freshly bloomed spring beauties alongside the also-edible yellow flower buds of glacier lily.

up after the snow melts, which varies by year and elevation. Find this plant on bare forest floors, between valleys, and in mountain meadows. Roots are best gathered from places where there is rich, nutrient-dense soil, as the roots will be bigger and worth harvesting. In habitats where this is not the case, take only stems, leaves, and flowers.

How to Gather

In some places spring beauty does not grow abundantly and has a meager root that really should not be dug up. Gather from older plants that have multiple stems growing from the tuber; let the younger plants continue to thrive. The rounded root, better known as a corm, needs gentle hands to uncover it. The stems will break easily if tugged, especially in rocky soil.

How to Eat

Spring beauty's succulent leaves and stems have a citrusy sweet flavor. Mince them for chilled gazpacho. Blend them with other foraged greens like wild onion and chickweed for topping crackers and cheese. Whole shoots blend well with other stir-fried vegetables. Flowers can be used to garnish cooked poultry or wild game. Roots of spring beauty can be used like baby red potatoes—when cooked, they are soft and melt in your mouth. The raw roots are crisp and starchy with a sweet flavor. Gathering enough for a meal is time-consuming, so blend them with other wild springtime roots to make the bounty last longer.

Future Harvests

Gather roots only where spring beauty grows abundantly and in rich soil. To be completely sustainable, clip only the aerial portions of this plant.

spruce

Picea species

mountain spruce

EDIBLE young tips, needles, resin

Spruce tips can be eaten raw and right off the tree in the spring for a citrusy chew full of vitamin C. Nibble small bits at first, to get accustomed to the new tart flavor.

How to Identify

Spruces are tall evergreen conifers, rising between 70 and 125 feet in height. Blue spruce (*Picea pungens*) and Engelmann's spruce (*P. engelmannii*) grace the Rocky Mountains, growing at elevations of 2,000 to 12,000 feet. These two trees can be hard to tell apart. Here are a few distinguishing factors. Blue spruce will be seen growing slightly lower in elevation, while Engelmann's can be found in higher forests.

Spruce tips at the perfect stage of harvesting, gather them just as the brown chaffy covering is ready to blow off.

Artisanal vinegars

Vinegar is an excellent medium for extracting minerals and vitamins from plants and a key ingredient in making homemade dressings, marinades, and condiments.

Fill a jar about halfway with the foraged herb or herbs of choice, and fill the remainder of the jar with a vinegar such as apple cider. Do not use raw or unfiltered vinegars. Let this herbal vinegar infuse for one to two weeks; shake daily, if you can remember. Strain, label, and store in the refrigerator. Your artisanal vinegar should stay stable for at least a year.

The numerous variations you can make with infused vinegars is exciting. Add honey to make the herbal vinegar sweeter, and you have something called an oxymel; use this combination for making simply superb salad dressings. Play around with different wild edibles to create your own unique dressing. Hawthorn-, elderberry-, or plum-infused vinegars could be added to make condiments like ketchup, barbeque, or sweet-and-sour sauces.

Spruce tips, juniper berries, and coriander seeds from the garden, infusing in apple cider vinegar.

Vinegars can be heated for better melding of ingredients, and sugar can be added to make vinaigrettes and reductions.

It's always wise to pack along a bowl for wild spring salads when headed out foraging. It is even wiser to have a bottle of homemade dressing, such as crushed shepherd's purse seed vinegars and olive oils like nodding onion or fir tip.

Both trees grow in a symmetrical triangular shape. Each species has branches that are loaded with short prickly needles. Each needle comes out of a tiny, woody peg on the branch; this is the best way to distinguish spruce from Douglas fir and the true fir trees. Engelmann's needles are much more flexible and not as sharp. Engelmann's has smaller cones that don't exceed 2 inches, while blue spruce has longer cones that will grow at least 4 inches. Engelmann's spruce can have hairy twigs. The needles of both species have a blue-green or silver cast to them. Some say that Engelmann's spruces have more of a camphor smell to the needles, while needles of blue spruce have a more pleasant lemony scent.

Where and When to Gather

You will find spruces in mixed conifer forests of higher elevations. Engelmann's is most common throughout the mountain west, while blue spruce is primarily in Colorado, Utah, and Wyoming. The tips of spruces can be gathered in spring. Look for the brown covering at the ends of the branches. This covering is a casing around the young tip; gather when these "hats" are plump and just beginning to blow off. Tips are best gathered while the needles are tightly packed but are still good when the tip reaches an inch or so long. Needles and resin can be gathered anytime of year.

How to Gather

Find an old conifer forest full of spruces or look to neighborhood trees—it's easy to gather plenty. Taste each tree, as the flavors can vary, especially if you happen to be in a mixed forest of both Engelmann's and blue spruces. Pick spruce tips from the branches with or without the brown casing. The casing can easily be removed from your harvest by rolling them between your fingers and letting it be carried off in a breeze.

How to Eat

Spruce tips, when fresh, are soft, chewy, and full of a zesty citrus flavor. Tips can be infused in local honey or olive oil, or blended into a flavorful finishing salt (see sidebar on page 179). Honey can be used for grilling, baking, and brewing tea. The infused oil is perfect on wild spring salads, adding a zest to the sometimes dull-tasting leaves. The tips simmered in water and sugar can create simple syrups for sprucing up soda spritzers or mojitos.

Try candying spruce tips by tossing fresh tips in the still-warm syrup and simmer for a few more minutes before straining them. Cover them with sugar, spread them out on a non-stick surface, and let them dry for a couple of days. Refrigerate or freeze the candies and use for decorative toppings. Spruce tips can also become a favorite of the home brewer, as it imparts a fruity, bitter taste to crafted beer.

How to Preserve

To make wild vinaigrette, fill a jar halfway with spruce tips, cover with a good dollop of honey, and add a few juniper berries, fresh stinging nettle tops, and wild onion flowers. Cover the remainder with apple cider vinegar. Get creative and include cracked pepperweed seeds, beebalm leaves, and a few smooth sumac berries from the stored bounty of the previous summer.

Future Harvests

Tree growth of spruce branches is slow, and harvesting the tips slows the growth of the branch even more. Luckily, spruces like to grow close together, making it easy to gather tips from many trees, merely pruning nature's garden. Do be conscious of young trees: let them be, and harvest only from the old greats that can spare a trim.

stinging nettle

Urtica dioica

nettle

EDIBLE shoots, leaves, seeds

It isn't spring until I get a sting from the stinging nettle patch. It is never just one, and I hardly mind. Stinging nettles are what real greens taste like—rich, earthy, and with a hint of mushroom.

How to Identify

Living up to its common name, stinging nettle can be identified simply by brushing up against it. The stinging hairs can be seen running up the stem, and all over the leaves. Technically known as trichomes, the hollow stingers hold formic acid and histamine, among other substances, which produce a stinging burn when contact is made with skin. The unpleasant feeling can last for hours and create small welts depending on how sensitive the person is. So before you go grab a plant that looks like a mint leaf, take a peek at the stem and underside of the leaf. If you see hairs, handle with care. Stinging nettle leaves are

Young emerging growth can be harvested by trimming off the top 3 to 4 inches.

Stop the harvest of stinging nettle leaves once the plant has gone to flower.

opposite each other and lanceolate, with serrations around the edges forming a pointed tip. Stems are square, thick, and can stand up to about 10 feet. Flowers are little, and hang in clumpy strands that dangle from the tops of the plant. Once they start turning to seed, the weight makes the plant bend over.

Where and When to Gather

Stinging nettle likes to be near some moisture, shade, and disturbed soils. Look near creeks, rivers, or wet fields. Reddish tops of the stinging nettle emerge first in the spring. Gather nettles throughout the spring and into summer, *before* they start to flower. Gather seeds in the fall.

How to Gather

Depending on your threshold for lingering stings or your agility level, you may or may not want to wear gloves. Wearing gloves and using pruners makes harvesting stinging nettles much more efficient and less painful. If you are in for the gamble, try pinching the stem of the plant with your thumb and index finger. The trick is to reach under the leaves from the bottom up, avoiding the opposite direction of the hairs.

A quick natural remedy, should any irritation result, is the juice from stinging nettle itself! Carefully roll up a nettle leaf in the same direction that the hairs are growing. This way you can cautiously use your fingers without being stung. After it is rolled up, fold in half and chew it up, then spit out the green poultice on to the itchy area. Or simply roll, fold, and squeeze between fingers to get some juice out, if the whole chewing thing is too much.

The reddish tops are the most nutritious and my favorite to dry for tea. Gather them when the plant is still young, snipping off 1 to 6 inches of the tender stalk. Snip heavy, hanging seed strands in late summer and early fall to dry seeds.

How to Eat

A soak in cold water for at least a few minutes before straining can make the stinging nettles easier to handle, lessening the sting. Even after soaking, eating nettles whole and raw is still not a good idea. The stinging action of the hairs deactivates when raw nettles are cooked or pureed. Stinging nettles can take the place of any tender cooked green. I love pureeing it, and mixing it with ricotta cheese as a filling for manicotti or lasagna. I grow nettles in my garden, so a few sprigs make it into most cooked dishes when the getting is good. Dried seeds can be used as a garnish as well.

How to Preserve

Dry stinging nettles for tea, or powder for a mineral-rich addition to beverages or foods. Most people say that drying the nettles eliminates the sting—not for me, only if its dried and powdered. When I dry the plant whole and go to grab a bunch or crush it with my hand, I get a reaction, so let it be known. Blanch and freeze whole or pureed nettles. Add to vinegars or honey for further blending in dressings, marinades, and desserts. Seeds can be collected and stored too.

Future Harvests

Stinging nettles are invasive perennial weeds in most areas, and there is no harm done to the plant by cutting off the tops. To extend your harvest, continue to clip off the top few inches, preventing the plant from flowering.

This plant will provide an ample amount of stinging nettle seeds.

stonecrop

Sedum lanceolatum

yellow stonecrop, lanceleaf stonecrop, spearleaf stonecrop

EDIBLE leaves, stems, flowers

Stonecrop may be the only plant greeting you on the craggiest mountain peak, offering you its juicy and refreshing leaves, with a taste reminiscent of cucumber.

How to Identify

Stonecrop is an ancient native plant that has sustained harsh mountainous climates for thousands of years. Its distinctive, juicy, green or reddish orange leaves grow tightly and alternately around the succulent stem, making them look like they are in a whorled arrangement. Leaves look like pointed nodules that turn from green to a burnt red once the plant flowers. The bright yellow, star-shaped flowers stand out, making this plant easy to see across hillsides in late summer.

The young shoots of stonecrop at the perfect stage for harvesting.

Starry, bright yellow flowers make beautiful floating garnishes for cocktails or spritzers.

Where and When to Gather

Sedum lanceolatum can be found all over the mountain west, enjoying its life on rocky hillsides, barely needing any dirt to cling to. Arid climates and harsh winters are preferred by this plant. It can be found growing at seriously high elevations and will sometimes be the only foliage around. Gather leaves and stems from this plant as soon as they are present in spring. Gather flowers in summer.

How to Gather

Stonecrop can take its sweet time to grow, so harvest only a stem or two from outcropping plants. Pinch or clip the stalk toward its base.

How to Eat

The entire plant can be eaten. Try the leaves and flowers raw in salads or tapenades. There is a slight mucilaginous component to the plant that is both refreshing and crisp, sort of like purslane but with more of a hint of cucumber flavor.

How to Preserve

Leaves and stems can be pickled in a variety of ways, as they stay firm and succulent.

Future Harvests

This plant is slow to spread, so gather only small portions from each plant and use sparingly. Cuttings can be transplanted easily, as this plant regenerates from where the leaf node and stem come together.

strawberry blite

Blitum capitatum

blite goosefoot, beetberry, strawberry spinach, strawberry goosefoot

EDIBLE leaves, flowers, roots

It's a weed with "berries"! It definitely depends on the soil this weed grows in, but some flower clusters really do have a truly fruity flavor—especially strawberry blite that invades your friend's fertile garden.

How to Identify

Strawberry blite starts out as a rosette of basal leaves, triangular in shape, like other goosefoot-family leaves; however, these leaves are more jagged, lacking the gray mealy coating that lamb's quarters and orache both share. The so-called fruit portion of this plant is actually a cluster of succulent flowers that produce small black seeds. Berries start out pale pink or yellow in color and mature into bright red fruit clusters. They resemble a morphed thimbleberry, but with black seeds that can be seen on the exterior. A distant relative of the beet, strawberry blite has roots that are likewise edible; they are marbled white with red overtones and look like a small parsnip.

Some red flower clusters are tasteless, while others have a mild sweet flavor.

A small bounty of the berry-looking flower clusters of strawberry blite.

Where and When to Gather

Strawberry blite is commonly found as a fugitive in garden beds, near a park bench, or by the compost pile. It has a naturalized habitat in the moisture-holding grounds of the mountains and foothills. Leaves are best gathered while young, in early summer, but can be gathered throughout the season. Flower clusters ripen in late summer and are best gathered when soft and bright crimson red with no light coloring left. Roots can be pulled up in early fall.

How to Gather

The young leaves of the rosette are tastiest and easy to gather by the bunch. The leaves thin out along the stalk (and become smaller as the plant ages) but are still desirable. The fruit-like flower clusters can be picked off the stalk like a berry. The taproots can be pulled or dug up. Obviously this kills the plant, so do this only if plenty of strawberry blite is growing nearby.

How to Eat

The whole plant has a bit of a nutty flavor. The leaves of strawberry blite can be eaten raw or cooked like spinach. Enjoy them raw on sandwiches or cooked on top of your pizza. Some berries taste very fruity, almost like a mulberry met a raspberry, with minimal tartness. The berries are most full of flavor when they are big, juicy, and crimson red. Pick them too young, and you may not like the taste. The ruby berries are fun to use in decorating roughage or fruit salads. Children love the red-staining fruit clusters, and gathering them is a great way to get young kids to participate in the garden. Roots can be enjoyed raw or cooked. They may not yield nearly as much as cultivated beets or parsnips, but they are worth adding for their sweet and crisp, beet-like flavor. Try roasting them with other root vegetables and add to soups or cold quinoa salad.

How to Preserve

The leaves can be blanched and frozen. I have heard of the berries being canned but have not tried this.

Future Harvests

If you want this plant to stick around in your garden, spread the seeds or make sure you leave a berry on each plant so it can go to seed.

Caution

This plant is high in oxalates, which, if consumed in large quantities, can cause gastric upset. Those with a history of kidney stones or who have a known sensitivity should proceed with caution.

sunflower

Helianthus annuus

EDIBLE flower buds, seeds

Wild sunflowers are much smaller than the cultivated ones but still provide us with the bounty of the succulent seeds.

How to Identify

Sunflower is the prime example of what its family members in the Asteraceae resemble. It has long yellow ray flowers emanating from brownish yellow disc flowers at the center. Plants are tall and branched, with oblong leaves growing alternately along the flowering stalk. Leaves toward the bottom are more heart-shaped and arranged opposite each other. All leaves and the stems are tough and hairy. Seed shells are black and contain the familiar beige-colored seed.

Sunflowers can be found growing in very dry and desolate regions of the mountain west.

Collect flower buds in summer, while they are still tightly closed.

Where and When to Gather

Sunflowers grow in clusters and are not often found alone. They inhabit disturbed soils up to about 9,000 feet. Sunflowers obviously enjoy full sun and will be found along roads, in fields, or pastureland. Gather tightly closed flower buds in midsummer. Seeds should be harvested when the flower has begun to wilt and the back of the flower has turned brown.

How to Gather

Buds can be plucked off. Cut the flower off the stalk and rub two seedheads together, or pick out seeds with your fingers.

How to Eat

The flower buds taste like artichokes. They can be boiled or steamed and served with herb-infused butter. If they are too bitter, try boiling them in a second change of water. Seeds can be roasted and salted in the shells or cracked open and eaten raw. They can also be made into a milk substitute, similar to almond milk, by blending with water and straining off the seedy pulp. The pulp can be utilized in baking or blended into granola.

How to Preserve

Store fresh seeds in a linen bag or open container to inhibit mold. Dried or roasted seeds can be stored in an airtight container or frozen.

Future Harvests

Sunflowers grow plentifully throughout the mountain west, sprouting easily from seed. Gathering the seeds and flowering buds will not hinder their growth.

Caution

Some people may have allergic reactions to plants in the sunflower family (Asteraceae).

sweet clover

Melilotus species

melilot

EDIBLE shoots, leaves, flowers, seeds

During monsoon season in the Rockies, rain comes every afternoon. At this time, the honeyed vanilla smell of sweet clover is left lingering in the air from one rainstorm to the next.

How to Identify

Sweet clover arises in various heights; it can be puny or quite tall. Leaves are alternate, light green, oblong, and serrated around the margins, with a trifoliate formation. Tiny yellow (*Melilotus officinalis*) or white (*M. albus*) flowers grow in slender spikes. Sweet clover resembles alfalfa (also edible) before it blooms, but alfalfa's blossoms are purple and its leaves are serrated only halfway around the margin.

Where and When to Gather

Sweet clover can be found in disturbed soils all over the mountain west. Some

Collect bundles of herb quickly from sweet clover's many flowering stalks.

Get ready to enhance your already creative cocktails! Both cordials and elixirs are made by infusing plant matter into liquor and adding a sweetener to cut the alcohol. Many plants and their parts—prickly pear, rose, sweet clover, young green black walnut hulls—make delicious liquor infusions. The herbs or fruit can be steeped in tequila, vodka, brandy, whisky, or whatever may be your preference. The alcohol extracts the flavors and aromatics of the plants; add a sweetener—like honey, maple syrup, molasses, or juices— and you have a cordial or elixir.

Start by filling a jar halfway with your herbs or fruit. Cover with your alcohol of choice. Keep stored in a sealed container for about a month, and shake when you remember. Afterward, strain out the plant matter and reserve your infused liquid. Add sweetener to taste. The alcohol will preserve your cordial or elixir for years. Try wild rose petal–infused tequila with a touch of maple syrup, or prickly pear– infused vodka.

roads are lit up with the bright yellow flowers for most of the summer. In drought, sweet clover is one of the first inhabitants of a starved reservoir's shoreline. The shoots can be gathered along with the young leaves in spring. The entire plant can be cut at the stalk once it is in flower or gone to seed.

How to Gather

After a few dry days, sweet clover is best to gather in the morning, once the sun has come up and evaporated any dew from the plant. Gathering plants while they are damp can cause them to mold, especially if the sweet clover is bundled before drying. It is best to spread the herb out on a drying rack immediately after collecting, or process it fresh right away.

How to Eat

Sweet clover is a stellar ingredient in baking and beverage-making. The vanilla essence it harbors is easy to capture, whether the plant is dried or freshly infused into a simple syrup or cordial.

How to Preserve

The scent of sweet clover is enhanced once it has been dried—that's when the vanilla-hay aroma really comes through. Make sure, if you are drying the leaves and flower for tea, that you gather on a dry day. This plant molds very quickly if wet when picked. Dried seeds can be stored and used as a mock vanilla flavoring that comes in handy as a sprinkle on yogurts, fruits, or ice cream.

The small yellow flowers of sweet clover can fill mountain meadows.

Future Harvests

Take as much as you want. Sweet clover is another plant that has made its way onto the invasive weed list; be mindful, however, that as a plant that fixes nitrogen in the soil, this "noxious weed" may actually be trying to heal the soil from which it is growing.

Caution

This plant contains coumarin. That's why sweet clover should never be gathered and bundled wet. When sweet clover ferments or the plant becomes moldy, coumarin can potentially turn into dicoumarin. This might be a problem if the plant is then eaten or made into tea and consumed in quantity. Dicoumarin prevents blood from clotting and could be seriously dangerous for those on blood thinners or for someone who has developed a bad wound in the backcountry.

Also, be careful not to confuse sweet clover with golden banner (*Thermopsis* species), a toxic plant with yellow flowers; golden banner has similar young leaves.

sweet root

Osmorhiza occidentalis
sweet cicely

`EDIBLE` leaves, flowers, seeds, roots

One of the first wild seeds to ripen, sweet root is usually chest-high, the perfect height to be spotted and gathered for its anise-tasting seeds.

How to Identify

Sweet root has mountain-hardy, lush green foliage. Leaves are compound in threes, pointed and serrated; some can be found along the stem, but many arise from the main stalk. Older plants have many flowering stems, reaching 4 feet tall; younger plants may have only a few and grow smaller, with more basal leaves.

Flowers are yellow, sometimes greenish, and hardly noticeable compared to the sizeable seedpod each becomes. Seeds are long, slender, smooth dark green crescents that are laterally flattened. Roots have a gray or brown surface and a light creamy-colored interior; they grow in what it seems like a tangled intertwined mess of rhizomes and roots.

Sweet root can have yellow or greenish flowers.

Gather the anise-flavored seeds while they are fresh and green.

Where and When to Gather

Sweet root dwells in forests, in mountainous terrain. It likes damp clean mountain soil and shade. It is an early-blooming flower, and the seeds ripen in early summer. Be sure to gather them early in that season, before they lose their taste. Roots of older plants are more aromatic and can be smelled just as the root is uncovered.

How to Gather

Pick an umbel full of green seeds. I find these pods lose a lot of flavor after they have been dried, so they are best enjoyed while fresh and early in the season. Leaves and flowers can be gathered as well. The root system is a large, aromatic tangle of rootlets. The sweet scent will stay in your house for days after it has been processed.

How to Eat

The leaves and flowers can be gathered fresh for salad greens or cooked gently to capture the delicate flavor. Fresh seeds can be ground into pestos or chevres for summertime guests. A sweet tea can be made from the green seeds and leaves; grind up the fresh leaves a little with a mortar and pestle to release the oils before steeping. Grating the fresh root is a great way to use only small amounts at a time for flavoring dishes with anise; too much root is really overpowering. The root should absolutely be used in a wild root soda or fermented beverages; it adds the flavors of licorice and sarsaparilla, with a tingly aftertaste.

How to Preserve

The whole plant is highly aromatic fresh, especially the root, which can be used to make infused liqueurs or dried for tea. The fresh root can be shredded or chopped and stored in the freezer for future use. I don't even bother drying the leaves, flowers, or seedpods anymore, as I have found them tasteless. Preserve the wild anise flavor in something sweet like maple syrup, simple syrup, or honey, for baking, marinating, soda-making, or finger-licking.

Future Harvests

Since this plant spreads through its root system, it's not a threat to gather seeds. But be conscious of your surroundings: take the whole plant only if sweet root is saturating the forest floor, and when harvesting the root, gather only from large stands. Rhizomes seem to transplant well. Dig up roots, and spread a few rootlets around the forest floor before you head home.

Caution

This plant is in the Apiaceae, meaning it contains deadly look-alikes. Water hemlock (*Cicuta* species) roots are odorless, but poison hemlock (*Conium maculatum*) can have a sweet celery-like scent. Sweet root has very aromatic seeds, leaves, and roots. Always make sure you are more than certain about the seeds you are consuming. A single seed of the wrong plant could be fatal.

tansy mustard

Descurainia species

leaves, flower buds, seedpods

In early spring these lacy-leaved plants will be springing up all over disturbed soils. Sample a taste of the budding flowerheads, and it will send you searching for more of their nutty broccoli taste.

My favorite part of tansy mustard to eat is the newest growth, the young budding clusters of flowers.

Tansy mustards grow tall with a cluster of yellow flowers and long, thin siliques.

How to Identify
The leaves remind me of ragweed, but tansy mustard is almost a foot tall in early spring and flowering, whereas ragweed will not be flowering until late summer. Flowers are small and yellow with the classic mustard-family traits of four petals and six stamens (four tall and two short). Leaves are lacy-looking and are covered in fine hairs; they are divided, toothed, and deeply lobed, and form pointed leaflets. The stalk is heavily branched. The thread-like seedpod, better called a silique, is only 1 to 2 centimeters long.

Where and When to Gather
Find tansy mustard in the dry lowlands of the mountain west. Gather tansy mustard in spring, in disturbed soils of places that are not sprayed. This shouldn't be too hard since parks and open lots seem to be loaded with these weeds in early summer. If the park sprays (hint: sprayed plants are yellow or brown, and deformed), look down the road to an open field that is not, and you will surely find tansy mustard. It will grow in any soil type, even contaminated ones, so do not be fooled into thinking the soil is okay just because tansy mustard lives there.

How to Gather
I prefer to eat just the budding flower-heads, as the leaves don't hold much flavor and can have a fuzzy, dry bite to them. Pick the flowerheads before all the yellow flowers are open.

How to Eat
Budding flowerheads have a taste that is nutty and similar to broccoli. Toss them into salads raw or quickly steam them for a spring side dish. Seeds have a nice mustard flavor and can be used as a spice this way. Blend them among other fresh mustard seedpods like pepperweed and pennycress for a wild mustard spread. Fresh seeds, flowers, and leaves can also be infused into oils or vinegars.

How to Preserve
Seeds can be dried and stored to be used as a spice.

Future Harvests
These plants have a very happy life in the mountain west. There is no way you can put a dent in that.

thimbleberry

Rubus parviflorus

EDIBLE shoots, leaves, fruit

Velvety smooth berries will melt in your mouth with a tart and sweet taste like raspberries, sure to bring you back for more.

How to Identify

Thimbleberries grow in thickets as a thornless shrub that reaches a few feet in height. You will never find just one thimbleberry plant because the roots spread as rhizomes, which is a good thing for the berry hunter. The leaves are large and palmate, with jagged edges around their five lobes; touch them, and you'll feel for yourself how soft and fuzzy they are. Flowers are big, white, and showy, resembling a white rose with five petals and many yellow stamens. Berries are deep red, and delicate, resembling a thimble when picked.

Berries have a velvety feel to them and are ripe when they are ruby red.

Some flowers have jagged tips on each petal, while others have entirely smooth petal margins.

Where and When to Gather

Thickets of thimbleberries are tucked in under the high canopy of conifer forests. The plant prefers shade but can also be found in sunny locations that are damp or close to a stream. Identify a spot in the early summer when the plant is in flower. This way you can come back in late summer when the other plants have overgrown your thimbleberry patch, and you'll know just where to look. Berries begin to ripen in August and can be found until early September. Another delight is to come back the following spring for the shoots and leaves of this plant. They are tart with a fresh astringent taste of roses.

How to Gather

Leaves can be gathered when they are young and tender, while they have a rose-berry flavor. Attempting to keep thimbleberries in one solid form while gathering—ever so carefully trying not to smash the berry while picking it off the core—is nearly impossible, so bring a glass jar and don't worry about the esthetics. It's easiest to put the berry straight in your mouth.

How to Eat

Despite the lack of durability as a fruit, it makes great fruit leathers and jams. Syrups, pie filling, ice cream, and other dessert-like treats can be made from the velvety berries. Be sure to use them that day, as they do not hold up well in the fridge for a next-day treat.

How to Preserve

Add thimbleberry mash into ice cube trays and freeze for quick additions to pancakes or muffins. A great way to preserve the fragile thimbleberry is blended into a vinaigrette or infused in vodka. Leaves can be dried for storage and used for tea.

Future Harvests

Pick your berry-loving heart out, and don't forget to drop a few for reseeding.

thistle

Carduus and *Cirsium* species

EDIBLE stalks

The problem with thistles is not how invasive they are but how much these plants are downplayed as a culinary delight. Their stalks combine a slightly sweet, almost melon-like flavor with the crispness of celery. Peel them for a sweet trailside munch.

How to Identify

Thistles are very spiny. Find spines all over the leaves, stalks, and even flower bracts. All will poke you, which may deter you from ever getting close to this plant. The leaves are sharply lobed or bipinnate, with

Nodding thistle (*Carduus nutans*) has large sharp bracts surrounding the bristly magenta flowerhead.

The emerging shoot of a thistle; notice the spiny leaves and stalk.

spines along the margins. Flowers are made up of many small disk flowers that form the blossoms of thistles; they are deep magenta or purple, popping out of green bracts that are round and spiny. Taken together, the flowers and bracts remind me of the bristles of an old-fashioned men's shaving cream brush.

Where and When to Gather

Find thistles anywhere the ground has been disturbed by humans. They grow well as invasive weeds in landscaped places, campgrounds, meadows, and pasturelands. The stalks can be gathered in late spring or early summer, before the plant has flowered.

How to Gather

Gather these plants with gardening gloves on; this will protect you from all the pokes and prods thistles have to offer. Chop the stalk at the base of the plant and begin peeling off the outer skin. The inner stalk can be used much like celery, eaten raw, or added into cooked dishes.

How to Eat

Though thistles may look a little intimidating to eat, they are actually delicious. Once

Elk thistle (*Cirsium scariosum*) has a cluster of flowerheads at the top of its thickly leaved stalk. This native grows throughout the mountain west, its silver-green leaves and shimmery spines glowing in the sun.

you get past the thorns, the edible interior of the stalk is crisp and quite substantial. Elk thistle has the largest stalk, and nodding thistle is well worth the peeling, too. Chop up the peeled stalk for cooking in sauces and soups, or add to vegetable medleys and stir-fries.

Future Harvests

Thistles spread easily and are rarely seen growing alone. Most are introduced species that can withstand overharvesting. Elk thistle, however, is a native plant and should be harvested only when there is a substantial stand.

Caution

Thistles are in the Asteraceae, and some people may have allergic reactions to this plant family. Also, some people—and I am one—get painful red stings from thistle spines. The stings may form slightly painful welts that last a day. Handle with care.

tumble mustard

Sisymbrium species

EDIBLE leaves, flower buds, seedpods

You would never guess, as they blow across the open road in late summer like a tumbleweed, that come spring, tumble mustard crowns and leaves taste like a gourmet salad green.

How to Identify

Tumble mustards grow tall and lanky, between 2 to 3 feet. They are easily identified in the spring by their dense basal rosette of jagged and deeply lobed leaves. These lower leaves are hairy around the margins, while the leaves that grow up the stalk can be hairless. As the leaves ascend the chaotically branched stalk, the lobes of the leaves become thinner and longer. Lower stems are hairy as well, thinning out to be hairless in the upper plant. The ends of the branched stems bear small, terminal clusters of light yellow flowers with four petals and six stamens. The silique, or seedpod, is slender and grows upward, to 4 inches long, looking like an extension of the stem.

Spot the jagged leaves of tumble mustards in a flat rosette on the ground in early spring.

A bowl of freshly cut tumble mustard florets awaiting the sauté pan.

How to Eat

The young leaves can replace arugula as a salad green or pizza topping. They have a similar flavor with a bit more spice. The leaves can be used to add more spice to cooked dishes. Do use them sparingly until you understand how much is needed to get the desired flavor. Flower buds and seedpods can also be used to flavor dishes, giving a distinct mustard burst. Use the young florets of tumble mustard like broccolini. I love them in a quick sauté of butter and garlic; they pair really well with juicy steak and mashed potatoes.

Where and When to Gather

Anywhere tumbleweed could drift to is where you will find this mustard happily planted. Plants prefer dry, rocky, and disturbed soils with full or partial sun. You will first see tumble mustard as a young rosette and not even recognize the same plant a month later, after it has bolted in height. Early spring is when you can identify the jagged basal leaves that are prime for picking; flower buds follow. Gather both through the spring. Seedpods can be collected from midsummer to fall.

How to Gather

The best parts of the plant are the young basal crown of leaves and young unbloomed florets. Pick leaves individually or cut the plant right above the root to get the full crown of leaves. Snap off the top 4 to 6 inches of the unopened flowerheads. Collect seedpods while they are still green.

How to Preserve

Store dried seeds in a sealed container for grinding into mustard powder or paste. Use these seeds for flavoring soups or sprouting, for a living winter snack.

Future Harvests

Tumble mustards are common weeds across the western states. As the dried stalk tumbles across the ground it disperses seeds, spreading them widely. Do not worry about taking most of the choice leaves and even the crowns when harvesting. Plants will continue to grow after being picked, and there are plenty around.

twisted stalk

Streptopus amplexifolius
claspleaf twisted stalk

EDIBLE shoots, fruit

I seek out the crisp shoots of twisted stalk as avidly as I would wild asparagus, if it grew in the mountains nearby my home. The stalks have a sweet taste that can be likened to cucumber.

The green berries will turn to red by summer's end.

How to Identify

Leaves of twisted stalk are almost rhythmically alternate, giving the stem of this tall plant a zig-zagged look; they are oblong-lanceolate, with distinct parallel veins and smooth margins. For every spot there is a leaf axil, a flower or eventually berry will be hanging below from a kinked stem. Flowers are white or yellowish green and have six tepals that arch upward. The berries, when ripe, are oval in shape and a deep orange-red, pink, or purple.

Where and When to Gather

Find twisted stalk close to creeks or streams that are flowing through moist mountain forests. It is best to identify a stand in the summer, while the plant is either in flower or beginning to fruit. This way you can come back the following spring, knowing exactly where to look and wait for the shoots to emerge. Berries can be picked in early fall.

How to Gather

Clip the young shoots at the base while leaves are still close to the stalk; shoots can be harvested as the leaves spread out, but the stem becomes tough as they grow tall. Pick berries just for a nibble. Twisted stalk berries are reported to have laxative properties if eaten in quantity.

How to Eat

Young stalks can be eaten raw or cooked. Try chopping up the young shoots for salads, or incorporate them in a frittata with other vegetables. Berries can be juicy, with a taste similar to watermelon.

Future Harvests

Gather the shoots only when there is a substantial stand, taking only enough for a small meal. In some places it grows with wild abandon, and there is enough to share with neighboring deer, who eat the greens, or grouse, who are fond of the berries.

Caution

This is a plant that needs 100% certainty when identified in the shoot stage, as it closely resembles the shoots of false hellebores (*Veratrum* species), highly toxic plants, which are usually growing close by. The leaves that surround the young shoots of young false hellebore are deeply pleated, a solid grayish green, and grow more plumply rounded than those of twisted stalk. The lower stem of twisted stalk often has a red tinge to it as well, whereas false hellebore remains a constant pale green.

veronica

Veronica americana
brooklime, American speedwell

EDIBLE leaves, stems, flowers

The leaves of veronica provide us with a crisp, slightly tart, spring-time dose of vitamin C, fresh from the cool running waters of the nearest clean stream bank.

How to Identify

Veronica is a creeping, matted plant that grows along and in the edges of creeks and rivers. Leaves are opposite, lanceolate, and serrated or entire around the margins; they are widest at the base, which hugs closely

Find veronica growing out of the creek water alongside watercress and wild mint.

The young leaves and stem of veronica have a reddish tint.

How to Eat

Younger leaves are less bitter and best used in salads. Older leaves can have a sharper bitterness, which may be enjoyed by some, or you could cook them to render them less bitter. Use them in sauces, stews, or soups. Veronica is high in vitamin C. This makes it a valuable green to the backcountry forager who is trying to incorporate more nutrients into their freeze-dried camping cuisine.

How to Preserve

Leaves can be dried or dehydrated. You could try blanching and freezing the fresh greens; though I have not tried this, I would imagine they shrink down considerably.

Future Harvests

As a bank stabilizer and water purifier, leave this plant to do its job, and take only little aerial portions from the top of the plant.

to the stem. In early spring, young leaves have a reddish tint; the rounded stem may be red, especially at branched junctions along the stem. Flowers grow on axillary racemes and are pale purple to blue, with four petals.

Where and When to Gather

Find *Veronica americana* growing alongside streams, bogs, or ponds, often with watercress and wild mint as companions. Harvest only from clean waters, gathering the young tips, leaves, and flowers from the plant in spring or early summer. All species of *Veronica* are edible and can be used interchangeably.

How to Gather

Gather the young leaves from the aerial part of the plant. The stem and flowers can also be used.

Caution

As with all water-living plants, be conscious of where you are gathering veronica. Do not gather in contaminated waters, and if the water is slow-moving or may run through some ranch land, take only the aerial portion of the plant. There is a very minimal chance of liver flukes; they exist in more humid regions, but livestock feces may contain them in any region. Simply do a vinegar rinse (see sidebar on page 274) if this worries you, or don't pick leaves on or below the water line.

violet

Viola species

EDIBLE leaves, flowers

There is nothing more refreshing in the springtime than gathering a wild salad bejeweled with violet blossoms.

How to Identify

The common name is a bit misleading. Not only do these plants come in violet but also yellow (*Viola nuttallii* and *V. orbiculata*), white (*V. canadensis*), and blue (*V. adunca*). A plant that always seems to hug the soil it grows in, violet is found blossoming from spring through summer. Flowers look complex: two matching petals arrange themselves on either side, another matched set radiates upward, and the fifth and largest petal points down. The fifth

A dense cluster of violet leaves makes a suitable harvest for a handful of salad greens.

Identify *Viola nuttallii* by its yellow flowers and narrow, lanceolate leaves.

petal displays the most beauty, varying in its color and shape from the other four and having deep-colored stripes that radiate from the center. The thick leaves of violets are usually heart- or teardrop-shaped; their distinctive veins give them an almost leathery appearance.

Where and When to Gather

Shade-loving plants, violets are found on forest floors in the springtime. This is the best time to gather, while they are in flower and hosting tender leaves. In mountain valleys, summertime is best for gathering; you can find them in places ranging from sunny meadows to aspen groves.

How to Gather

It is best to use a pair of scissors or small pruners to gather leaves and flowers. Sometimes pinching the leaves can result in uprooting the entire plant. Some species are more elusive than others, so respect them all and gather only a few flowers and leaves from each plant.

How to Eat

Viola flowers add a certain splendor to any beverage or meal. Candy them or use them to make tea, infuse honey, or adorn cupcakes, muffins, and other baked goods. Our native violets are unlike their aromatic sister *V. odorata*, which you will primarily

Viola nephrophylla has purple flowers and rolled, heart-shaped leaves.

find in tidy garden beds. Our wild violets do not hold the classic violet flavor of *V. odorata*. Leaves have a touch more mucilaginous texture to them than the flowers, especially when cooked. Young spring leaves are best for use as a salad green. When leaves are more mature, boil them until they become tender for an addition to a side dish. Greens can be used to thicken soups or stews.

How to Preserve

Blossoms can be frozen in time by placing individual flowers into each compartment of an ice cube tray filled with water. Drying the leaves and flowers together makes a nourishing and demulcent tea for the winter months.

Future Harvests

Pick with delicate fingers. Please do not go ripping this plant out of the ground.

watercress

Nasturtium officinale

EDIBLE leaves, flowers, seedpods

Watercress is one of the few greens that can be harvested year-round, even from unfrozen creeks in the dead of winter.

How to Identify

Watercress is a water-loving plant. You can distinguish it by its bright green foliage and tiny white flowers that form mats in streams and along riverbanks. Leaves are shiny and deeply lobed. Each lobe has a match on the other side of the midrib, and a large lobe heads off the end of the leaf. Flowers grow in clusters and hold the staple four petals of the mustard family (Brassicaceae), shaped as a crucifix. Seedpods are long and rounded.

Watercress differs from water hemlock (*Cicuta* species) by having flowers with only four petals that do not grow in an umbel shape. Watercress leaves are more broadly lobed, creeping over the water.

The rounded green patches in the water are colonies of watercress, fresh for the picking.

Where and When to Gather

Watercress inhabits slow-moving waterways. Never gather watercress where there are heavy pollutants or stagnant water. Never pick downstream from livestock farms or polluted waterways. Gather creekside in clean water all year long.

How to Gather

Between the possibility of liver flukes (see caution) and the fact that most nearby waterways with watercress are invariably flowing through a cow pasture, I always take extra precautions when gathering this plant. I bring clippers and take *only* the leaves, flowers, and seedpods that are above water.

How to Eat

Watercress has the perfect tones for a wintertime green. Its spicy mustard flavor can be enjoyed cooked into watercress soup or as a bed of greens for cooked salmon. Add the leaves to sandwiches, puree into a spread, or enhance salad dressings. Seedpods add a crisp spicy bite to salads and stir-fries.

How to Preserve

Blanch and freeze leaves for an addition to soups or lasagnas. Watercress makes an excellent infused vinegar. It can also be dehydrated in the oven for a few hours at 130 to 145 degrees Fahrenheit and stored dried.

Future Harvests

Do not pull watercress out by its roots; it protects stream banks and beds from erosion, and you want to ensure that it stays where it is.

Caution

Poisonous water hemlock (*Cicuta* species) can be found growing very close to watercress; be certain of the leaves you are collecting. Submerged watercress stems could harbor the larvae of liver fluke (*Fasciola hepatica*), a nasty parasite that can cause liver damage. If you are picking aerial leaves of the plant only, not those in the water, then larvae should not be present, as they need water to live and cannot climb. If you are still worried, a vinegar rinse will kill liver flukes—or just cook your watercress: heat kills.

wax currant

Ribes cereum
desert currant

EDIBLE fruit

A small red berry, wax currants have a subtle taste reminiscent of fruit punch, which is not a flavor you expect in the arid Rockies.

How to Identify

Wax currant berries grow on a broad bush with small fan-shaped leaves, similar to other *Ribes* leaf patterns. The foliage differs by having smaller, minuscule lobes spanning the rounded edge, and a waxy aromatic coating can be felt on the leaves. Flowers—long, whitish pink fairy trumpets—hang open toward the ground. As the ovary swells into a berry, remnants of the flower sepals remain at the tip of the berry, serving as a reminder of the delicate flower it once was.

Where and When to Gather

Wax currant loves the strain of rocky slopes, withstanding direct sun and a lack of water. It can also be found at the edges of forests in partial shade. It grows in open sagebrush lowlands, sunlit canyons, on

The leftover, dried flower tail of wax currant makes them easy to tell apart from other red berries.

Berries are small, earthy, and sweet. They take on the taste of the forest and can sometimes carry notes of pine.

hillsides, and atop cliffs. Berries can be found ripening in midsummer, and a few may still be clinging into the fall, if the birds missed them.

How to Gather

Some bushes are more loaded than others, and some tend to host sweeter berries, too. Grab a branch and use a raking hand method, combing the berries off the branches with your fingers and catching them in a bucket or basket. Alternatively, put a tarp or blanket beneath the bush while you shake vigorously, letting the berries collect on the blanketed ground. Clean berries in a bucket of water: they sink to the bottom, making it easy for you to skim off the floating debris.

How to Eat

Freshly plucked berries are nice and remind me of a bland, not-so-sweet fruit punch. Berries can be cooked into sauces or they can be blended into oil or vinegars for dressings and marinades. Cooking down the berries first makes the best jellies, fruit leathers, and marmalades.

How to Preserve

Marmalades, jellies, jams, marinades, syrups, infused alcohol—all can be made from these berries, but jazzing them up with other wild berries is best to enhance flavor.

Future Harvests

Help spread seeds by scattering berries as you eat them off the bush.

western blue flax

Linum lewisii
wild blue flax

EDIBLE seeds

Ground flax seeds can be added to an assortment of meals for a nutty flavor and huge nutritional boost.

How to Identify

The many flowering stems of western blue flax arise from a single woody root crown. Many short, thin, linear leaves grow alternately along each stem. Five-petaled periwinkle or blue flowers sit atop the wispy stems from late spring to midsummer. Bowl-shaped seedpods can be seen in summer; a single plant will bear dozens of seedpods, each with many dark seeds inside.

Where and When to Gather

Western blue flax grows all over the hills of the mountain west. Find it mixed in among other wildflowers in mountain meadows, grasslands, or sagebrush swales. Gather in late summer when the seedheads are dry.

Western blue flax blossoms and buds.

How to Gather

Never gather seeds while they are still green; this is when they harbor a lot of cyanide. Harvest seeds only when they are darkened. Gather the seeds on a day when it has been dry and sunny for the previous few. Cut the stalks at the base and make bundles of your harvested plants. Let your plant bundles dry hanging over a sheet or screen, in case seeds start to fall out. After about a week the seeds will easily come off by shaking or rubbing the seedheads into a bucket or bowl. A lot of chaff will come off with this, so winnow your seeds into another bowl.

How to Eat

The seeds of western blue flax contain fiber, omega-3 fatty acids, vitamins, lignin—to name just a few nutritional players. Flax seeds can be eaten raw, roasted, sprouted, or ground. Ground seeds have optimal nutritional value, as the unchewed seeds will just pass through your system. Flax seeds are a useful ingredient in egg- or gluten-free baking, as they have a gelatinous texture that binds well. They are a great addition to home-made crackers, piecrusts, muffins, or biscotti.

How to Preserve

The best way to store raw flax seeds is to dehydrate them on the lowest setting after your harvest; seeds will keep for up to three years if stored in an airtight container. Roast flax seeds by placing them in a dry, non-stick pan over medium heat. Stir continuously for three to five minutes or until the seeds become fragrant. If you are worried about cyanide consumption, this is a good way to ensure the least amount. Flax seeds should be ground only prior to use, as the powder goes rancid quickly even when stored in the refrigerator.

Future Harvests

Takings seeds from multiple plants will not make a dent in populations.

Caution

Cyanide poisoning from the raw seeds is possible only if you are strictly eating an unbalanced diet of plants containing cyanogens. In this unlikely case, the concentration of cyanogenic compounds can build up and store in the body, which may then lead to life-threatening conditions.

white clover

Trifolium repens

EDIBLE leaves, flowers

White clover is a common low-growing plant whose leaves and flowers make a nutritious addition to salads, soups, and teas.

How to Identify

White clover can be recognized by the tiny white pea-like flowers that make up the flowerhead, which sometimes carries a pink hue. Each individual flower of the blossom is small and tubular in shape, carrying a drop of nectar at the base. This low-growing plant has trifoliate leaves, and many of them bear a white or light green chevron marking. White clover rarely exceeds 10 inches in height and spreads by stolons, just like wild strawberry.

Light-colored chevrons often mark the leaflets of white clover.

Where and When to Gather

White clover can be found almost anywhere the sun is shining. A creeping plant, it is often the primary ground cover in fields and meadows. Flowers bloom all summer.

How to Gather

Trim the leaves and flowers back on a sunny, dry day. Gathering damp leaves and flowers makes them not suitable for drying, as it can promote mold. When drying leaves and blossoms, lay them on a screened drying rack.

How to Eat

Blossoms have a subtle sweetness of sweet peas when cooked into dishes such as quiche or tossed raw into salads. Both the leaves and blossoms are rich in minerals and nutrients, making them a great herb to add to soups, sauces, and stews. Bone broths can include fresh white clover and other herbs, such as red clover, stinging nettle, and northern bedstraw, to provide even more nourishment.

How to Preserve

Dried blossoms and leaves can be stored in an airtight jar away from sunlight to maintain maximum freshness. This dried herb can then be used for nourishing infusions. Increase the nutrients in cooked rice or pasta by adding a handful while the water boils.

Future Harvests

White clove is an abundant perennial plant that is very resistant to harvesting and even mowing. It would be next to impossible to overharvest.

whitetop

Lepidium draba

hoary cress, draba

EDIBLE leaves, stalks, flower buds, flowers, seedpods

One of the spicier wild mustard greens around, whitetop is a weed worth getting to know. Green seedpods can be used for stone ground wild mustard.

How to Identify

In spring the basal leaves can be identified by their steely blue-green hue, which comes from the tiny white hairs coating the young leaves. Flowers are white, each with four petals; they are arranged in

Find the spicy greens of whitetop in midspring.

Gather the closed flower buds and stalk for a tasty sautéed vegtable.

flat-topped clusters. Alternate leaves hug the central stalk closely; they are oblong and sometimes toothed. Seedpods are rounded or heart-shaped and contain one or two brown seeds.

Where and When to Gather

Whitetop, a sun-loving invasive, grows from 3,000 to 8,500 feet throughout the mountain west. Growing by means of a horizontal root system, it spreads quickly in disturbed alkaline soil, especially in places near farmland, where adequate water is supplied through irrigation. It is one of the first perennial weeds to sprout in the spring and is often targeted for spraying: don't harvest from deformed or yellowing plants! Young leaves can be gathered from the basal rosettes in mid- to late spring. Gather the budding flowering stalks before they bloom in April and May. Blooms fluctuate depending on elevation. Gather green seedpods in summer.

How to Gather

I pay most attention to whitetop while it is putting forth its budding stalk; clip 3 to 4 inches off the top of each stalk. Leaves that grow on the budding stalk can be left on while cooking. While the plant is in full bloom, cut the stalk low to the ground.

How to Eat

The young budding stalks make the perfect broccolini substitute. Spring basal leaves, flowers, and green seedpods can be used in salads for hints of mustard. Older leaves are more pungent and mustardy (some people find they leave a lingering, not-so-pleasant aftertaste) and go a long way if you're using them in cooked dishes, but chopping up a few older leaves finely and adding them to salads is quite delightful, with each bite having a hint of spice.

How to Preserve

Wild mustard can be made with varying seeds of different species in the family Brassicaceae. Try a blend of pepperweed, whitetop, and pennycress.

Future Harvests

This plant appears on noxious weed lists throughout the mountainwest, so you can harvest with impunity.

Caution

Since this plant takes over areas quickly and is considered a noxious weed, do be careful not to harvest from a sprayed area. Also, it has been indicated that hydrogen cyanide may be present in young leaves in very small amounts, but it is completely removed in cooking.

wild caraway

Carum carvi

EDIBLE leaves, flowers, seeds, roots

This exotic spice, bearing flavors of the Far East, is now growing as a mountain west weed in a neighborbood near you.

How to Identify

Caraway is usually a biennial plant, putting out basal leaves the first year and flowering in the second (and sometimes a third) year. Leaves of caraway look like a mix of carrot and yarrow; they are arranged alternately

Wild caraway is a biennial plant, meaning it will not flower the first year but will have basal leaves.

Cattle graze meadows full of wild caraway's white umbel flowers.

up the flowering stalk. The stalks grow 1 to 3 feet tall, putting forth white or pinkish flowers arranged as a flat-topped umbel. Stalks can be green, straw-colored, or purple-tinged; they stand tall from a small taproot that can be up to ½ inch thick. The seeds (technically achenes) of wild caraway are highly aromatic, crescent-shaped, slender and brown, with linear ridges that are lighter in color.

Where and When to Gather

Wild caraway can be found near water, in woods or open fields, at elevations up to 9,000 feet. Finding a spot where pastures are nearby is often a good area to look. Collect leaves and taproots in late spring and early summer. Gather flowers in summer, when present. Seeds are ready by late summer or early fall.

How to Gather

Collect the drying achenes directly from the stalk of wild caraway. Gathering can be easy in large areas; cut the stalk just under the umbel, or use your fingers to take some off the tops. Sift through, keeping only the fruits; let them dry out for a few days in paper bags.

How to Eat

Add leaves, flowers, or seeds to your salad. Roots can be used for their sweet parsnip flavor in cooked dishes. Use the achenes as a flavorful garnish to roasted vegetables or meats. Mix them into your favorite baked goods, such as homemade rye bread, for that staple cumin-fennel flavor. The achenes also make a great addition to ferments like sauerkraut, or may be used to infuse vinegar dressings. Spice up your rice pudding or curry with crushed or whole fruits. In eastern restaurants, you may see

Fresh wild caraway seeds are full of flavor.

a bowl of caraway seeds to take on your way out as an after-meal digestive aid. A simple tea can be made from powdered or crushed achenes.

How to Preserve

Dried caraway achenes can be stored for months, maintaining their flavor throughout. The taste can be preserved in your favorite pickled or canned foods. Grind up as a powdered herb to add to the spice rack or for making tea.

Future Harvests

In Colorado wild caraway is considered a noxious weed and is required to be eradicated, contained, or suppressed, so why not take all the "seeds"?

Caution

As with any carrot-family member, you must be 110% on your identification of the plant you are seeking. This plant family contains two of the most deadly plants in North America. Water hemlock (*Cicuta* species) and poison hemlock (*Conium maculatum*) are both white-umbelled flowers, as is wild caraway. Ingestion of either hemlock can be fatal, as it was for Socrates, who in 399 BC drank a potion of conium that ended his brilliant life.

wild chives

Allium schoenoprasum

EDIBLE leaves, flower buds, flowers

Inhale! A field full of wild chives is a scented watercolor, with edible brushstrokes of sleek leaves and onion-flavored pink flowers.

How to Identify

Wild chives are smaller than the garden variety but identical in characteristics, with pink-purple flower blossoms and long, slender green leaves. Star-shaped flowers bloom in a dense inflorescence atop hollow scapes (stems). Leaves are also hollow, smooth, pliable and almost soft to touch. Bulbs are small, slender, and oblong in shape. It is hard to tell one variety from another with wild chives and to know if the plant was introduced or is native (*Allium schoenoprasum* is both, as it happens).

The densely clustered purple flowerheads of wild chives sit atop long, thin, hollow stems.

When cooking, pick the fresh flowerheads apart to spread out the savory spice or use them whole to heat a dish up.

Where and When to Gather

In the height of the summer, wild chives can be found glittering moist mountain fields. Escapees from gardens turn up around neighborhood alleys, in parks, and bordering trails. Gather leaves and budding scapes in late spring and continue harvesting from the plant through summer.

How to Gather

Wild chives provide such nice long leaves and voluptuous flowerheads that the bulb really doesn't need to be bothered. Scissors or clippers can be used to cut back leaves and budding or flowering scapes.

How to Eat

Use any part of the fresh plant. I love eating the flowerheads of chives raw; they are full of a perfect spice, so positively sinus-clearing that I can eat only one at a time. The flowerheads make a beautiful floating garnish for martinis and mojitos. Leaves and scapes are divine in mashed potatoes, on top of tea sandwiches, or garnishing deviled eggs. The bulbs are small but can be used in place of store-bought onions when cooking.

How to Preserve

Apple cider vinegar infused with wild chives, stinging nettles, and red clovers is a mineral-rich vinegar. Try drizzling it on crisp summer cucumber and dill salad or use as a base for marinade. Simply stuff a jar with your wild bounty about halfway, pour in the apple cider vinegar, and add a plop of honey for a touch of sweetness or cracked pepper for some spice. Finely chopped leaves and budding or flowering scapes can be dried and stored as a spice. Try making your own wild *fines herbes*, a French combination of herbs that includes chives, tarragon, chervil, and parsley. Use wild chives and mountain parsley, and sub in sweet clover for tarragon and sweet root for chervil.

Future Harvests

Harvesting leaves and flowers should not hurt the success of this plant, as it is a perennial, but always let some buds or flowers stay behind for reseeding.

Caution

The young leaves of death camas (*Toxicoscordion venenosum*) and mountain death camas (*Anticlea elegans*), both extremely toxic and inedible plants, could be mistaken for the grass-like leaves of *Allium* species. Be certain with your identification.

wild grape

Vitis species

leaves, tendrils, fruit

Wild grapes may be shockingly smaller than their cultivated kin, but what they lack in size, they make up for in intensely tart flavor.

How to Identify

Big palmate leaves with three lobes and jagged edges grow on these woody, sprawling vines. In a quest for more sunlight, wild grapes scramble all over trees, taller shrubs, and anything else onto which they can latch their forked tendrils. When in bloom, clusters of small green flowers give

Hearty wild grape leaves shrouding the trunk of a tree.

way to a lovely aromatic scent. Wild grapes are deep purple when ripe and each fruit contains two to six seeds.

Where and When to Gather

Frost grape or riverbank grape (*Vitis riparia*) can be found in the eastern Front Ranges of Alberta, Montana, Wyoming, and Colorado. Canyon grape (*V. arizonica*) can be found mostly in the southwestern mountain west, including Nevada and Utah. Mapleleaf grape (*V. acerifolia*) is the least common in the mountain west, occurring only in parts of southeastern Colorado. Grape vines can be found sprawling along forest floors, hovering over the banks of waterways, and climbing trees. Wild grapes love the cool shelter of shaded places and moist soil. Gather leaves and tendrils in late spring. At that season, the leaves are big and still pliable; once the veins have firmed up, they become harder to use as a wrap. Clusters of grapes ripen in late summer and early fall.

How to Gather

Leaves, tendrils, and clusters of grapes can all be snapped off the vine by hand or cut with scissors.

How to Eat

Before wild grapes fruit, the tendrils provide a nice tart chewing "stick." These are best fresh, as they lose their sweet-and-sour flavor upon drying. Wild grapes can be quite bitter, but freezing them or letting them chill in the refrigerator overnight seems to soften the tart bite. If eating them fresh, do be mindful that the wild varieties contain noticeable seeds. Grape juice is easily made by heating up the wild grapes in just enough water to cover them and boiling them for about 10 minutes while mashing. The skin and seeds can be strained off; sugar or more water can be added to level out taste. Grape jelly can be made from grape juice by adding pectin and sugar.

Wine can be made from fresh or cooked wild grapes. Take precaution with raw grapes as the tartrate in the juice can irritate the skin when being processed (see caution).

Dolmas (from the Turkish, *dolma*, "stuffed") are a common Middle Eastern dish and have been a favorite of mine since childhood. Grape leaves wrap the fillings of vegetables, rice, or meat, making a nice snug roll.

How to Preserve

Ever see a grape leaf floating in a pickle jar and wondered why? The tannins in the leaves help keep fermented or pickled items crunchy. The leaves can be blanched and frozen for future use. Grapes can be frozen on or off the stem to be eaten later, but leaving them on the stem can make picking them off easier when you want to process a whole bunch. Grape jelly and wine can be made when the harvest is bountiful.

Future Harvests

When taking leaves, tendrils, and clusters, try not to rip down the growing vines. Be sparing with the leaves by not stripping a vine of them all.

Caution

Be certain with your identification of wild grape, as it does have poisonous look-alikes, such as false Virginia creeper (*Parthenocissus vitacea*), which has very similar-looking fruit but distinctly different leaves: leaves of false Virginia creeper are pinnately compound with five leaflets.

Some people find fresh wild grape juice to be irritating to the skin or the stomach, if processed or drunk in quantity. This is due to the presence of tartrate, which can leave a burning sensation on the skin. Use gloves if you are mashing up a bunch of raw grapes by hand. Tartrate can be rendered once the grapes are juiced. Remove the tartrate by letting the juice sit for a few days, and the tartrate residue will sink to the bottom. The top portion of the juice can be decanted off, leaving the residue behind. Fresh grape juice can then be made into wine, canned, or frozen, and no future irritation will be encountered.

wild hops

Humulus lupulus

hop vine, golden hops

EDIBLE shoots, leaves, strobiles

The sedating effects of hops can be felt in beer and from the bitter brew of tea.

A fresh tangle of wild hops.

The deeply lobed leaves are rough to the touch

How to Identify

Wild hops grow from a creeping bine, not a vine, as plants do not have tendrils, suckers, or hooks, but instead use stiff hairs and a vigorous stem to climb bushes and other natural trellises. As a perennial plant it dies back in the fall and grows again the following year; each year the bine will reach quite impressive lengths of 10 to 40 feet. Leaves are either heart-shaped or have large lobes, usually three to five, and are finely toothed, growing opposite one another. *Humulus lupulus* is dioecious, meaning there are separate male and female plants. Both plants are needed for pollination. The female flowers, or strobiles, look like small, soft, green pinecones. The male flowers hang in loose panicles that grow 3 to 5 inches long.

Where and When to Gather

Wild hops grow throughout the mountain west, and indeed, North America, in open meadows, disturbed soils, and forest edges. Still, it might be good to start with a place you know hops are going to be returning, or finding them could prove to be a challenge. Gather the shoots in early spring. Gather young leaves later that season and into early summer, before they mature and become rough and tough. Strobiles are ready for harvesting in late summer and early fall.

How to Gather

Shoots are ready for plucking when they are a few inches tall. The young leaves will be ready to harvest shortly after this or at the same time. Simply pluck a few from each plant, leaving plenty behind for photosynthesis. The strobiles are ready to be picked when they are highly aromatic and vibrant in color; get them before they dry out. Pick them from the stem and place in a paper bag to keep all the lupulin. A fine golden powder will be present on the strobiles or in the bag after harvesting; this resinous powder is the lupulin, the source of this plant's sedative and calming effect.

How to Eat

Add the shoots to anything for their unique asparagus-hop-like flavor; try them in soups, steamed or sautéed atop risotto, and scrambled into your favorite egg dish. Young leaves can be eaten raw or mixed in among other wild sautéed greens, adding a bite of bitterness; obviously, we can use their citrusy aromatics in fermented beverages such as beer and ales.

How to Preserve

Dry strobiles out of direct sunlight to preserve the freshness of the buds; they hold up well dried for concocting calming and sedative teas. Shoots can be pickled with spices, vinegar, and even the addition of beer, such as an IPA or stout for flavor. Pickled hop shoots are a long-standing delicacy in Belgium. They can replace a pickled asparagus in a Bloody Mary or be used as a pizza topping.

Future Harvests

No concerns here, beyond the usual: never strip any one plant of all it offers the forager. The bines are weather resilient and can be transplanted easily through spring cuttings.

wild lettuce

Lactuca species

EDIBLE leaves, stalks, flower buds

Wild lettuce is one of the most bitter springtime edibles, but when chopped and tossed with other foraged greens it adds a welcome, even pleasant bite.

How to Identify

The leaves along the stem are lanceolate and held alternately, clasping closely around the stalk. Leaf margins are toothed or prickly and may or may not be lobed. The underside of the midrib is barbed.

Wild lettuce is best distinguished from other edibles with milky white sap (chicory, dandelion, sow thistle) by the barbed midrib on the underside of its leaf

Other similar-looking plants, like chicory, dandelion, or sow thistle, lack these small spines; however, all these plants—wild lettuce and the three aforementioned—have a milky white sap. The flowers of wild lettuce are yellow with prominent green bracts. Wild lettuce can have a lot of branched flower stems coming off the main stalk. Seeds are small, brown, and attached to a fluffy white pappus.

Where and When to Gather

Wild lettuce is a weedy foe to many in the mountain west, as it grows just about anywhere its seeds land. Find it in vacant lots and fields or lining sidewalks and parking lots. Gather the young leaves of the basal rosette in early spring and into summer, until the plant puts up a flowering stalk. You may also collect the young stalk and unopened flowerheads in summer.

How to Gather

Pick off the choice-looking young leaves from the young rosette. Cut the stalk off at the base while it has flower buds on it.

How to Eat

Wild lettuce is bitter, but remember bitter is good, as it aids in digestion. You may have to adjust your taste buds a bit to appreciate the flavor. Your body will surely thank you for incorporating it into your diet. Start by adding small amounts to your fresh green salads, by chopping it so that you do not get large bites of it. The young budding flower stalks can be used in salads as well; steam and butter the young stalks for a side-dish nibble.

Future Harvests

Feel free to harvest vigorously—it's even fine to pull this easily spreading weed from the ground.

Caution

Wild lettuce is in the Asteraceae, and some people may have allergic reactions to this plant family.

wild licorice

Glycyrrhiza lepidota

licorice root, American licorice, sweet root

EDIBLE shoots, roots

The sweet root of this North American native perks up any wild tea. Try a brew of wild mint, rose, and wild licorice—they should all be growing relatively close to one another.

How to Identify

The long leaves of wild licorice are compound and pinnate, always with an odd number of leaflets. The lanceolate leaflets grow opposite each other with a single leaflet at the tip. Leafstalks have a slight downward bend to them that deepens on hot days. A sticky, waxy coating can sometimes be felt on the entire plant. Wild licorice grows about 2 feet tall and forms robust colonies, thanks to its creeping root system. It has elongated white clover–shaped flowers that bloom in late spring and remain through summer. Flowers are primarily white but can be yellow-green or purple-tinged at times. Wild licorice is commonly confused with poisonous milk vetches (see caution), but the fruit of wild

Wild licorice can easily be pulled up when growing in the disturbed soils it prefers.

Flowers of wild licorice are white and sometimes with hints of purple.

licorice is brown and burred. It is the only member of the pea family (Fabaceae) in the mountain west that has this spiny fruit.

Where and When to Gather

Find wild licorice colonies skirting around cities, towns, and mountain drainages throughout our region, near mountain streams and irrigated fields and ditches. Gather shoots in spring. Gather roots in either spring or fall, which is when they hold the most flavor.

How to Gather

If gathering roots in the spring, utilize the young shoots as well; they are tasty raw. The large taproots may be hard to dig up, as they can reach 3 feet in length; therefore, choose a location that has loose soil, such as a riverbank. In some places, roots are easily pulled up, complete with attached rhizomes, which can also be consumed.

How to Eat

Young spring shoots can be eaten raw in salads, used in smoothies, or slightly cooked. Slow-roasted licorice roots are sweet and fleshy, with a flavor reminiscent of sweet potatoes. Roots can also be used to flavor cordials or liqueurs.

How to Preserve

Roots can be chopped up finely for drying and used in an infusion or decoction. Fresh or dried roots can be simmered for a few minutes in water to make a strong decoction and drunk as tea. Wild licorice makes a fine addition to tea blends in small amounts: besides having a knack for pulling flavors together, it adds a hint of sweetness and a soothing demulcent note. Turn the root into powder before adding it to teas that will be made into water infusions.

Future Harvests

This plant is stout and an aggressive grower; harvesting some roots should not hurt the stand. Don't harvest in areas where wild licorice is a bank stabilizer, helping to keep down erosion. Rhizomes transplant well and have been known to take over gardens.

Caution

Wild licorice has a look similar to milk vetches (*Astragalus* species), which are poisonous; be positive with your identification. Not for use in pregnancy, or by people with high blood pressure or kidney disease (wild licorice causes sodium retention).

wild mint

Mentha arvensis

peppermint, poleo mint, field mint, cornmint

EDIBLE leaves, stems, flowers

My fondest wild mint memory? Sitting in a mint-laced hot spring with my love. We boiled water on an adjacent camp stove, added mint to our mugs, and sipped the peppermint-flavored tea while we soaked.

How to Identify

Mentha arvensis, our most common mint species, is almost always growing at water's edge. I pick what I think is a mint leaf—simple and in opposite pairs—crush it, and take a sniff. Mint will always smell like mint, and all mint stems are square. For certainty's sake I roll the stem, feeling for the ridges of a square; I then pop some leaves in my mouth. The flowers grow

Light purple ball-like clusters of flowers decorate the stalk of wild mint.

Gathering wild mint along the bank of a stream at dusk is always magical, especially when one of my favorite foraging companions has "come with."

around the stalk and look like light purple puffballs; flowers are small with long stamens.

Where and When to Gather

Along streams and riverbanks is a good place to start, when looking for wild mint. Anywhere there is substantial moisture and a bit of shade is where you will find mint from spring into fall. Young leaves are more tender; they get tougher and less potent as they age and begin to brown.

How to Gather

Walking along a riverbank or in a moist field, you can usually gather more than enough mint bundles. I pinch off the top 4 inches of the plant, leaving plenty of leaves and flowers behind.

How to Eat

Mints make the blandest beverages or edibles come to life. Try adding mint to your skunkbush or smooth sumac lemonades or mix it in among bitter, bland, and spicy wild greens. Mint tea is marvelous dried or fresh, although fresh has such an enhanced flavor.

How to Preserve

Bundle your mint by tying string around the base where you pinched the stems, and hang with the fresh top pointing downward to let dry. Or you could pick leaves off of a fresh stalk one by one, but I find it easier to gather a bunch, let it dry, and then crush off all the dried plant matter for tea.

Future Harvests

Do not go tearing mint out of the soil; it acts as a stabilizer, protecting banks from erosion. Be gentle while harvesting this plant, and always leave enough for regrowth.

wild plum
Prunus americana

EDIBLE fruit

Wild plums are decadently sweet, and they can be strewed and stewed for scrumptious desserts, spreads, sauces, and brews.

How to Identify

Thickets of happy, haggard plum trees lace the canyons and roadsides of lower-elevation ranges. Wild plum often looks more like a hardy shrub than a tree, with thinner trunks covered in peely, prickly gray bark. Flowers are fragrant, with five white petals, and blossom in late spring. Wild plums ripen from green to a reddish orange or purple and are about half the size of their commercialized cousins. A plum is a stone fruit, meaning it has a

Ripe plums can be found from late summer into the fall.

A stout and craggy wild plum tree.

single pit. The flesh surrounding the pit is dark yellow and juicy when ripe.

Where and When to Gather

I love going to the Front Range of the Rockies in late summer or early fall, when the fruits are abundantly adorning these small trees. From Colorado to Canada, it's impossible not to stop and load up the dashboard of my truck. Also find this plant dispersed through Utah, in parts of the western side of Montana, and into the panhandle of Idaho. Gather in places where you are away from the road or pollution; the trees need adequate rainfall to produce fruit. Look for them near riverbanks, in ravines, or small couloirs where rainwater funnels.

How to Gather

Find a loaded tree and taste a plum before picking a whole bunch. Some can be quite astringent and bitter or not very juicy at all. Fruits are often best after the first frost, which makes them super ripe and sugary. I pick one by one and toss into a big basket; the softer they are, the sweeter the fruit.

How to Eat

Some plums are better than others right off the tree. Find a few good-tasting trees, and you will have a sufficient store of fruit. When processing many plums at one time for jams, leathers, or sauces, cook down the whole fruit with some water and remove the pits by pouring the pulp over a quarter-inch screen.

The inner nut of the pit is edible as well, but eat only a few raw, as they contain small amounts of cyanide. Crack open the pit to find a tiny nut that resembles an almond. The nut can be roasted to render the cyanide. Smash up the nuts and cook the mash down with a little water to extract the bitter-almond flavoring. Cooking also removes the cyanide. Use the bitter-plum-nut extract as you would bitter almond in baking.

How to Preserve

Wild plums can be preserved every which way: jelly, syrup, dried, fruit leather, fermented wine, and sauces. To dry plums, slice plums in half, remove the pit and let the fruit dry or dehydrate on a low temperature.

Future Harvests

If the plums are there for the taking, take them.

wild rose

Rosa species

EDIBLE flower buds, flowers, fruit

Don't let a few thorns keep you from harvesting fragrant rose blossoms. Pick the buds starting in late spring or pluck petals into summer for infusing their sweet floral essence in teas, honeys, and syrups.

How to Identify

The fruits of wild rose are called rosehips; when ripe they are deep red, round, and plump. Thorny thickets are recognizable throughout the year, thanks to either the lingering red rosehips or the heavenly scented flowers. Flowers range in size and color but are always a shade between a white or dark pink; they have five petals, five sepals, many stamens, and a deep yellow center. Leaves grow alternately as pinnately divided leaflets. Each leaf has

Remember to leave behind some rosebuds and flowers in spring and summer if you plan on coming back to gather hips.

Rosehips can be found well into the winter; some will still be soft and sweet, while others suffer from the elements.

one to four pairs of leaflets, with a single leaflet at the tip. All leaflets are ovate in shape and serrated.

Where and When to Gather

Roses can be found in many areas of the mountain west, along waterways, on craggy mountainsides, or at the edges of willow, poplar, and conifer forests. Rosebuds and the flowers that follow can be gathered as soon as you see the pink petals swelling inside the green sepals. Rosehips can be gathered into the dark days of winter and are usually one of the only fruits remaining.

How to Gather

Bushes will have flowering roses and budding flowers at the same time. Rosebuds can be plucked and dried. Rose petals can be picked off individually by gently

pinching all five petals from the calyx. Be sure to gather on a dry, sunny day, which will provide you with the most aromatic flowers. Rosehips can be munched on at any time (but see caution). They are definitely best after the first few frosts. Frost helps to sweeten up the tangy flavor and soften the flesh.

How to Eat

One can never have enough rose petals or buds dried and stored. Rosebuds are my favorite for tea, as they seem to impart the most flavor; find your own perfect flavor, but I suggest three to five buds per cup of water. Rose hydrosol can be made from the petals of fresh or dried roses; this water can be used as a flavoring for cocktails, champagne, and desserts or as a tonifying facial spritz. Rose petal or rosehip syrup also makes for a lovely soda or sorbet. The fresh petals and buds can be candied to decorate muffins, cakes, and cookies. Fresh petals and hips can be infused in vinegar for a salad dressing, or for marinades.

How to Preserve

Rose petal jelly not only provides a treasured spread for baked goods and brie but also delivers impeccable flavor to lamb, glazed on either before or after cooking; combine with apples for their pectin and complementary flavor. Wild mint and fresh rosemary also pair nicely in a wild rose jelly. Rose petals can be cooked at a low heat in butter for a delectable spread that should be kept in the freezer.

Ripe rosehips can be placed in a jar and covered with honey. Once covered, mash

How to make a hydrosol

A hydrosol is the aromatic essential oils of a plant, captured through condensation and infused in water. You can make a hydrosol by heating an herb in a covered pot of water. To do this, you need the right setup: a pot large enough to contain the herb, the water, and two bowls (or one bowl and one brick!); some ice to create the condensed steam; and a lid that can be turned upside down while still fitting snug, containing the vapors. The upside-down lid should have a nice concave shape to it; this lets the hydrosol run to its center and drip into a bowl that is propped up out of the water (use another bowl or a brick for the pedestal). The ice will be placed on top of the upside-down lid. I find it easiest to use leak-proof bags of ice, where you can pour out the water as it melts and refill the bags with ice.

The herb water should be heated to a simmer and kept covered for 30 minutes to an hour before you slowly lift the lid to check how much hydrosol has been collected. When lifting the lid, make sure to tilt it in such a way that the water condensation run off into the bowl of hydrosol—don't lose a drop.

Keep hydrosol stored in the refrigerator. Use in place of water in baking or add to cocktails. Makes a nice facial spritz, too!

the hips to impart more of the hibiscus-like flavor. Let this infused honey sit for about a week and then strain well before use. Rosehips are not only delicious but also high in vitamin C and can be made into jellies or marmalades as well.

Future Harvests

Roses are very common in the mountain west. Gathering the buds, petals, and hips will not do any damage to a bush's habitat and growth; however, routinely stripping your favorite bush of buds will mean no hips later in the season.

Caution

The very fine hairs attached to the seeds of rosehips can irritate the throat or digestive tract, causing diarrhea in some cases. I find that if I strain my rosehips well when they are infused in honey or tea, I am not bothered. Alternatively, slice open the hips and scrape out the seeds and hairs before eating or preserving.

wild strawberry

Fragaria species

EDIBLE leaves, flowers, fruit

It's always a treat to turn over strawberry leaves and find a cluster of red gems. Wild strawberries are a small yield, but their taste is deliciously concentrated. You will cherish each berry.

How to Identify

Wild strawberry grows horizontally, sprawling across the ground bearing white flowers and three-parted leaves. The leaflet edges are evenly jagged, giving them the distinctive strawberry look. Fine hairs may be present on the underside of the leaf and along the leafstalks. Five white petals make up the delicate flower that turns to fruit by midsummer. The stems of the fruits, flowers, and leaves are sometimes red, making them easy to spot.

Where and When to Gather

Strawberries dwell in meadows of varying elevations. They like moist but not wet soil and are often surrounded by plants that won't completely crowd out sunlight. Find

Strawberries are one of the first plants to flower in spring.

Look low to the ground come summer. When the strawberry fruits, it hides its berries beneath its own foliage, protecting them from the rays of the sun.

them near forest edges and riverbanks and along trails. Leaves and flowers can be picked in the spring. Berries can be gathered starting in early summer and continuing until late summer at higher elevations. They may grow bigger at lower elevations, and flavor can be dependent on habitat, but the tiny morsels at 11,000 feet are worth the scavenge.

How to Gather
Crouching low to the ground, turning over leaves, and finding clusters of sweet berries is the only way I know how. Make sure to have a sturdy container on hand, as this will help keep these delicate wild berries intact.

How to Eat
The all-time best way to enjoy wild strawberries is on the spot, by the handful. If you can get a good amount back to your home, add them to any baked good or your favorite yogurt, or take a crack at making your first ice cream, sorbet, or fruit leathers. Add leaves and flowers to wild salads or enjoy as a tea.

How to Preserve
Berries are very tiny once dried, but they remain a minuscule treat: add them to chocolates or trail mix. Mash strawberries and freeze fresh in ice cube trays for additions to beverages. Jam, syrups, and liqueurs are another way to savor the summer flavor of strawberries all year long.

Future Harvests
Strawberries spread vegetatively, by stolons, sending out stems that produce new plants. In other words, there's no need to worry about overharvesting this fruit. The only concern is that the birds and bears may get to your stash first.

wintercress

Barbarea species

yellow rocket

EDIBLE leaves

Winters in the Rockies can be brutal, but this arugula-tasting mustard plant is up to the challenge. One of the most resilient greens, wintercress can be found year-round, if not covered by snow.

How to Identify

The basal leaves of wintercress, arranged in a rosette, look like a bundle of arugula greens sprouting from the earth. Leaves are darker green than arugula but sport the same large lobe at the tip of the leaf, with smaller lobes descending to where the leaf meets the central stalk. Atop the tall red-streaked green stalk are yellow flowers blooming in clusters; they have four petals and six stamens (four tall and two short), the telltale sign of a plant in the mustard

The flowers of wintercress are a bright yellow marker of tasty greens to come.

Young leaves bear a resemblance to arugula, but they are rougher and spicier, with more of a bite.

family (Brassicaceae). Two species grow in abundance in the mountain west, *Barbarea vulgaris* and *B. orthoceras*. They are very similar, and you may not be able to tell them apart until they have gone to seed: *B. orthoceras*, our North American native, has smaller, blunter siliques.

Where and When to Gather

Wintercress is a sun-loving plant that will also tolerate partial shade. Look for it in disturbed areas that are near water or hold good moisture. If you mark a spot before the snow comes with a stick, you may be able to have a harvestable winter salad green. If strategic planning isn't your thing, then spring will do just fine. It is best to gather from this plant before it sends up its flowering stalk, as thereafter the greens get tougher and are not as big.

How to Gather

Leaves can be picked one by one, or the whole rosette can be grabbed at the base

while you cut back some of the leaves. I always give the plant some respect and don't take them all. Even invasive weeds deserve a chance at a full life cycle, if I have a say in it.

How to Eat

Wintercress mixes well with tender salad greens that may be somewhat lacking in flavor. Use only a few sprigs when cooking, as wintercress can be overpowering. Start by sautéing small amounts in butter or oil and adding more to taste, until you achieve the desired flavor intensity.

Future Harvests

Common wintercress (*Barbarea vulgaris*) is considered an invasive weed; however, American wintercress (*B. orthoceras*) is a native plant and should be respected as such. Since it is hard to distinguish between the two, treat both equally. For this reason, do not uproot the whole plant to get leaves.

Wolf's currant

Ribes wolfii

western currant

EDIBLE fruit

Enjoy the tart berries of Wolf's currant while out hiking mountain trails, or take some home: their bold flavor is even nicer when combined with sweeter ingredients.

How to Identify

Wolf's currant is a thornless, branching bush that can reach 5 feet in height. Its white flowers, star-like and saucer-shaped, grow in a densely clustered terminal raceme. Leaves are lobed (they look like small maple leaves). The glandular berries are rough-looking and bristly to the touch;

The starry white flowers of Wolf's currant grow in a clustered spike.

Berries begin green, turn red, and are nearly black when ripe.

they start out green, but like so many gooseberries and currants, they turn dark purple–blue or almost black at maturity.

Where and When to Gather

Find Wolf's currant in subalpine forests, along mountain creeks, and sometimes mixed into the shrubs of the alpine tundra. Gather berries in late summer or early fall. Ripe times for berries will depend on how high you are in elevation. Berries that grow at a higher altitude will ripen later in the season than those growing in lower regions.

How to Gather

Clip off the clusters of berries and process the berries at home. Remove the berries from the stem by gently running your fingers along it, popping berries off. Or if it is easier, remove the berries one by one while in the woods.

How to Eat

Wolf's currants can be enjoyed straight from the bush for a refreshingly new taste on a long uphill hike. Add to your camping assortment of food: toss some in oatmeal, or smash them into your peanut butter and jelly sandwich. Once you have brought a small bounty home, use them fresh or dried in pies, muffins, or cakes. Cook down the berries into mash for fruit leathers, or strain out and add sugar for simple syrup.

How to Preserve

Berries can be dehydrated or frozen for future use.

Future Harvests

Picking berries of Wolf's currant will not impact the future success of this alpine-loving shrub, but make sure to leave some behind for the animals of the high country.

wood sorrel

Oxalis species

EDIBLE leaves, flowers, seedpods

It may not be a patch of lucky clovers or taste quite like Lucky Charms, but this sweet, tart-and-tangy plant is one to be discovered and loved.

Wood sorrel can be stepped over and missed because it grows so low to the ground.

The five-petaled flowers and banana-shaped seedpods of wood sorrel.

How to Identify

At first glance you might think you are looking at a patch of clovers, but upon further inspection you will see the tiny five-petaled flowers and small, elongated green seedpods. Leaves do resemble those of a clover, bearing the same three symmetrical leaflets, joining together at the central point of the leafstalk; however, wood sorrel's leaflets differ by having a very prominent heart shape and a defined crease at each of the midveins. At night the heart-shaped leaflets fold up along the crease, and even during the day you may find some this way. Flowers are usually yellow (*Oxalis stricta*), less commonly purple (*O. violacea*). Seedpods have a cylindrical shape; they taper to a point facing skyward, resembling teeny-tiny upsidedown-growing okra.

Where and When to Gather

Wood sorrel is found growing in shady places that are well watered; it could be in a moist forest, around buildings in cities, in a shaded portion of a garden, or in campgrounds and other disturbed soils. A good time to gather the leaves of this tart, lemony-tasting plant is before it flowers, as they are most tender and subtly sweeter then; however, leaves can be gathered all spring and summer, while plants are simultaneously flowering and fruiting.

How to Gather

The entire plant is edible and easy to snatch. Leafstalks and stems can be a little stringy to swallow but are pleasant to chew on and spit out. If you want to avoid the lower stalks altogether, grab plants at the base and gently strip the leaves, flowers, and seedpods right off.

How to Eat

Add the leaves and seedpods to a leafy green or fruit salad for flavorful little bursts of lemon, rhubarb, and sour apple. The seedpods are fun for wee ones to gather and munch on like little sour candies. Wood sorrel can be added to soups or sauces for its acidic flavor. A tart, refreshing beverage can be made from the fresh plant by chopping it up and infusing it in water for several hours. Strain out the plant matter, and serve the drink chilled on a hot summer's day.

How to Preserve

I suppose ice cubes could be made from the infused water and kept captive for a tart winter's drink. Infuse butter or oil with wood sorrel for future cooking by sautéing the plant over low to medium heat for a few minutes. The infusion can be kept in the fridge for a few weeks or frozen.

Future Harvests

It is probably best not to yank up stands of wood sorrel. Since it is a fragile plant, use gentle fingers to take only the aerial portions of the plant.

Caution

This plant contains small amounts of oxalic acid. Do not eat large quantities if you are malnourished or have kidney problems.

yarrow

Achillea millefolium

milfoil, plumajillo

EDIBLE leaves, stalks, flowers

Yarrow flowers and leaves make a lovely aromatic tea. They are the perfect warming drink to sip on while sitting next to a fire on a chilly end-of-summer night.

How to Identify

Yarrow is a native perennial averaging heights of 1 to 3 feet. Plants can have one to several stems that arise from long basal leaves; some stems may themselves be branched, and the leaves along the stem are small and especially feathery. Both basal and stem leaves are distinctly aromatic when crushed. Flowers form clusters that appear to be in an umbel; however, upon closer inspection you will find several separate flower clusters in heads, which form a flat-topped corymb.

Where and When to Gather

I am fairly positive I can find yarrow almost anywhere in the mountain west. Gather leaves as you need them from spring

The tightly closed buds and fragrant white flowers of yarrow. Note that distinct clusters of flowers make up the flat-topped corymb.

The deeply dissected, fern-like leaves of yarrow are highly aromatic when crushed.

through fall. Stalks and flowers are best gathered while the flowers are at their most fragrant, in the heat of the midsummer.

How to Gather

Gather leaves by plucking a few from each plant. If snipping off the whole stalk to use along with the flowers, it is best to first strip the stem of leaves, then chop up the stalk finely, leaving the flowers still attached.

How to Eat

I have used yarrow flowers to decorate salads and baked goods. This is not a plant that I add to culinary dishes, but it is an herb that I love to sip on as a tea; it is warming and bitter, making it the perfect non-alcoholic aperitif after a heavy dinner. Yarrow can be added to cocktail bitters for its bitter aromatics.

How to Preserve

Hang bundles of gathered flowering stalks to dry. After they have dried, crumble the leaves off the stalks if they were not stripped earlier and break apart the flower clusters. Stems can be cut up into tiny pieces and stored along with the other foliage. Store in a sealed container for a few years, and the herb should still be potent. To check, take a whiff or chew on the dried herb to see if it still holds its bitter aromatics.

Future Harvests

Yarrow is widespread throughout the mountain west; always leave some flower-heads behind, and never strip a plant of its leaves.

Caution

Yarrow is in the Asteraceae, and some people may have allergic reactions to this plant family. What's more, yarrow is often confused with water hemlock (*Cicuta* species) and poison hemlock (*Conium maculatum*) because its white-flowered corymb resembles an umbel. Be positive of your identification.

yucca

Yucca species

stalks, flower buds, flowers, seedpods

The young flower stalk of yucca bears a surprisingly close resemblance to asparagus and tastes similar when roasted.

As it emerges, tho flower stalk of yucca looks like a large asparagus shoot among the sharply pointed leaves.

The edible flower buds and blossoms of yucca.

How to Identify

There are not many plants in the mountain west that look anything like yuccas. They are a distinct evergreen presence year-round—their tall brown flower stalk and long green spine-tipped leaves can even be seen protruding through the snow. There is usually only one flower stalk per plant, and the rosette of leaves pokes out around its base. Leaves are stiff and sword-like, with fraying fibers along the edges. Flowers are bell-shaped and creamy white, with tints of purple or green. Oval seedpods are green or cream-colored.

Where and When to Gather

This plant can be found throughout the lower and middle elevations of the mountain west, usually below 8,500 feet. It prefers the harsh climates of the desert, lack of water, and long, cold winters, growing among junipers, piñons, and ponderosas. The young flower stalk looks like a giant asparagus and can be harvested in spring. In early summer the flowers can be found budding and blossoming along the stalk. In late summer the seedpods are green and ready for gathering before they brown.

How to Gather

The emerging flower stalk can be sliced off a few inches from the base; be careful of the sharp leaves. When gathering flowers, I like to take a nibble of the bud or a petal first, before I consume a lot: raw flowers have made my throat tighten and feel itchy (see caution). Seedpods can be plucked off the stalk. Fruits of soapweed yucca (*Yucca glauca*) and Spanish bayonet (*Y. harrimaniae*) are hard and fairly bland, but those of banana yucca (*Y. baccata*) are soft and sweet.

How to Eat

Raw or cooked, the buds, flower petals, and young green seedpods can be incorporated into many different dishes. Flower petals are an edible garnish; try them as a floating delicacy in soups or cooked into omelets or stir-fries. Young stalks can be roasted or boiled and, if necessary, peeled to uncover the tasty inside. Young fruits can be cooked in a variety of ways; try battered and fried or stuffed and baked.

How to Preserve

Flower buds can be dried and stored for later use. Young green pods and young stalks can be pickled.

Future Harvests

Harvesting from several plants will do no harm. Don't take the lone flowering stalk from a lone yucca.

Caution

Eating too much of this plant has been known to have a laxative effect—how much seems to vary from person to person. Some people get ill effects from the plant raw. It will depend on the species you are working with. Boiling or cooking the plant parts removes the potential for ill effects.

Metric Conversions

Inches	Centimeters		Feet	Meters
1/4	0.6		1	0.3
1/3	0.8		2	0.6
1/2	1.3		3	0.9
3/4	1.9		4	1.2
1	2.5		5	1.5
2	5.1		6	1.8
3	7.6		7	2.1
4	10		8	2.4
5	13		9	2.7
6	15		10	3
7	18			
8	20			
9	23			
10	25			

Temperatures

degrees Celsius = 0.55 × (degrees Fahrenheit – 32)

degrees Fahrenheit = (1.8 × degrees Celsius) + 32

To convert length:	Multiply by:
Yards to meters	0.9
Inches to centimeters	2.54
Inches to millimeters	25.4
Feet to centimeters	30.5

Useful Resources

Foraging wild foods is a hands-on journey that requires the right resources. My guidance has come from botanical teachers, field guides, plant keys, and the inspiration from other wild foodies' experiences. My knowledge of wild foods has come from direct interaction with the plants that live near and far from my home in the Central Colorado Rockies. Here is a list of references I have used in the past, resources I suggest you check out, and plant guides to help you in your identifications.

Wild Food References, Resources, and Guides for Identification

Elpel, Thomas. *Botany in a Day: The Patterns Method of Plant Identification.* Pony, MT: HOPS Press, 1996.

Elpel, Thomas. *Foraging the Mountain West.* Pony, MT: HOPS Press, 2014.

Kershner, Bruce. *National Wildlife Federation Field Guide to Trees of North America.* New York: Sterling Publishing, 2008.

Lesica, Peter. *Manual of Montana Vascular Plants.* Fort Worth, TX: Brit Press, 2012.

Marrone, Teresa. *Cooking with Wild Berries and Fruits of the Rocky Mountain States.* Cambridge, NM: Adventure Publications, 2012.

Moore, Michael. *Medicinal Plants of the Mountain West.* Santa Fe: Museum of New Mexico Press, 2003.

Morgan, Liz Brown. *Foraging the Rocky Mountains: Finding, Identifying, and Preparing Edible Wild Foods in the Rockies.* Guilford, CT: Morris Book Publishing, 2013.

Schofield, Janice. *Discovering Wild Plants: Alaska, Western Canada, the Northwest.* Bothell, WA: Alaska Northwest Books, 1989.

Seebeck, Cattail Bob. *Best-tasting Wild Plants of Colorado and the Rockies.* Englewood, CO: Westcliffe Publishers, 1998.

Seebeck, Cattail Bob. *Survival Plants of Colorado.* Drake, CO: Cattail Publishing, 2012.

Thayer, Samuel. *Nature's Garden: A Guide to Identifying, Harvesting, and Preparing Wild Edible Plants.* Birchwood, WI: Forager's Harvest, 2010.

Thayer, Samuel. *The Forager's Harvest: A Guide to Identifying, Harvesting, and Preparing Edible Wild Plants.* Ogema, WI: Forager's Harvest, 2006.

Weber, William, and Ronald Wittmann. *Colorado Flora: Western Slope.* Boulder: University Press of Colorado, 2001.

Williamson, Darcy. *The Rocky Mountain Wild Foods Cookbook.* Caldwell, ID: Caxton Press, 2011.

Plant Identification and Location Websites

bonap.org

plants.usda.gov

Websites and Blogs of Wild Foodies

arcadianabe.blogspot.com

cauldronsandcrockpots.com

eattheweeds.com

fat-of-the-land.blogspot.com

foragersharvest.com

honest-food.net

hungerandthirstforlife.blogspot.com

ledameredith.net/wordpress/

the3foragers.blogspot.com

wildfoodgirl.com

wildmanstevebrill.com

Acknowledgments

I am so appreciative of my patient and supportive husband. My son and he have encouraged me every step of the way, especially when I am moving slow on a hike because of my constant plant grazing and collecting. I am grateful to be able to share my passion for wild edibles; however, I would be nowhere without the knowledge gained from a community of plant-savvy individuals, and that includes authors, bloggers, and the natives to our land. It is their willingness to share the culture of wild food gathering that keeps this learned information alive.

My craft of seeking through the woods and gathering botanicals to eat and use has been led by many plant-wise people. I would like to thank all my teachers, colleagues, students, friends, and family, who have embraced the love of wild edibles and herbs with me. I would like to especially thank Lisa Rose for her never-ending companionship and mentoring as I tackled writing this manuscript, as well as jim mcdonald and all the other herbalist and foragers that are a part of a growing intertwined web.

I give so much gratitude to the written works of wild food authors like Thomas Elpel, Cattail Bob, and Sam Thayer.

Many photo credits go to Kimbre Woods, who was dragged out into the field with me in rain, snow, and sunshine. I am thankful for her expertise and always-willing attitude. Also, many thanks to my brother-in-law, David Allen, who provided me with the photos I could not get to in the northern Rockies; Max Licher, for his beautiful photos from the southwestern quarter of this region; and Erica Marciniec of wildfoodgirl.com, for the capture of alpine sorrel.

I so appreciate my in-town editor, Jamie Wilkins, who provided me with invaluable guidance throughout my writing process. I was fortunate to work with herbalist and botanist Katherine Mackinnon, who spent hours ensuring my botanical descriptions were clear and concise. My editors at Timber Press, Juree, Eve, and especially Franni, have been wonderfully supportive and a pleasure to work with. Thank you for your continued support.

And last but not least, I would be nowhere without my wandering giant sidekick of a dog, Bella. She always takes me further than I want to go. She continually seeks out wild treasures I may or may not be seeking.

Photography Credits

David Allen, pages 12 (top right), 63, 270, 271, and 288.

Max Licher, pages 12 (bottom right), 93, 117, 134, and 232.

Erica T. Marciniec, page 39.

Lisa Rose, pages 12 (bottom left) and 133.

Kimbre Woods, pages 12 (center right), 23, 35, 54, 64, 71–73, 105, 123, 145, 146, 186, 191, 194, 220, 237, 239, 241, 242, 269, 277, 310, and 317.

All other photos are by the author.

Index

About the Author

KIMBRE WOODS

Briana Wiles is a wild plant expert who loves expanding people's knowledge about the plants surrounding them. She teaches foraging and medicinal plant classes out of her home and locally in Gunnison, Colorado, and runs a small herbal business, Rooted Apothecary, which offers her own line of body care products made with foraged botanicals. She resides in the central Rockies of Colorado with her husband, son, and Alaskan malamute. In her spare time, she enjoys rock climbing, snowboarding, hiking, boating, and figuring out how to forage while doing the aforementioned. Visit her at rooted-apothecary.com.

12   301